FREE TRADE, FREE CANADA:

how free trade will
make
Canada stronger

Also by Earle Gray
IMPACT OF OIL (1969)
THE GREAT CANADIAN OIL PATCH (1970)
SUPER PIPE (1979)
THE GREAT URANIUM CARTEL (1982)
WILDCATTERS (1982)

FREE TRADE, FREE CANADA:
how freer trade will make Canada stronger

EARLE GRAY
editor

ISBN 0-9693400-0-1

Published by Canadian Speeches
PO Box 250, Woodville, Ontario, K0M 2T0, Canada

Printed and bound in Canada

CONTENTS:

FOREWORD

Free trade, free Canada.

That sums up why the free trade agreement with the United States must be approved.

Free trade means freedom for initiative and enterprise; freedom to grow, freedom to prosper. It means freedom to work, with more jobs available. It means more freedom of choice, with more goods and services available at less cost. It means that our children and grandchildren, instead of having to move elsewhere in search of larger opportunities, will be freer to seek their career goals here in Canada. It means freedom to help ourselves, and others too. Everyone benefits from trade. The freer it is the more we all benefit: Canada, the United States, the third world.

Free trade means we can be even more Canadian, more independent, more sovereign. The more we earn, the more we can afford for Canadian art and culture, education and research, social assistance, and programs to resolve regional economic disparities.

The Canada-U.S. free trade agreement can't be the end of the quest. It's only a start. It isn't perfect. It doesn't give us all the opportunity we deserve. It doesn't, by itself, open the doors to freer trade with other nations. It doesn't fully protect us from protectionism — either American protectionism, or even Canadian protectionism.

But it's a step in the right direction. It's something that we can build on, extend, and improve in our trade with our largest partner. And it's a banner that can leads us on a crusade for freer trade with the rest of the world.

The alternative to free trade is restricted trade. That means less freedom, less opportunity, less growth, less prosperity, less money for social programs. It will mean more government intervention and control over business, our jobs, our lives. In the 1930s, restricted trade meant impoverishment and world war. We must turn aside from that path with the Canadian-U.S. free trade agreement. We must take this step in the right direction.

More than 20 years ago, as editor of Oilweek magazine, I had advocated free trade with the United States as the only feasible way to secure assured U.S. markets for Canadian energy. Now, opponents of the free trade agreement argue that it will sacrifice Canadian control over the export of our oil, gas, uranium, and electricity. What they really mean is that the resources of Atlantic Canada, Quebec and the west should be put on hold so they'll be available to Ontario at less than market price, while Ontario-made cars and other tariff-supported products are sold at more than market price. It is the same issue that has created more regional strain and tensions in Canada than anything else, with the possible exception of English-French relations.

As editor and publisher of **Canadian Speeches,** it struck me that the most forceful arguments in support of the free trade agreement were being expressed in hundreds of speeches across the country. Assembling the best of these between two covers, it seemed to me, offered a unique opportunity for a more powerful expression of the essential benefits of this agreement than could be made in any other way.

In **Canadian Speeches** we have already published the text of a number of speeches in this debate, both pro and con. But it is not the purpose of this volume to present both sides of the argument. Arguments of the opponents to this bilateral trade agreement have been strongly voiced in both print and broadcasts, more strongly, perhaps, than the arguments of the advocates.

The purpose of this volume is to present a shared viewpoint that is held with passionate conviction by people who care about Canada.

For the sake of credibility in dealing with an issue so controversial, it seemed essential to me that this book should be prepared and published with no financial support from any firm, organization or government agency — not even the Canada Council. No such support has been either sought or offered.

Earle Gray
Woodville, Ontario
March 1, 1988

PART ONE:
THE HISTORY, 1846 - 1986

Chapter one:
the question that won't go away

Other than our sometimes fractured relationship of French and English speaking peoples, Canadians have been arguing longer and louder about free trade with the United States than any other issue in our history.

We've been arguing out loud about it for nearly a century and a half, and the arguments today are exactly those that have raged since 1846. They pose a question that ultimately every Canadian must decide: do you want to join the United States?

While the basic argument in the debate over free trade versus protection — and especially free trade with versus protection from the United States — have not changed, events have yielded a bumper crop of contradictions, ironies and paradoxes:

• The actors in the drama have changed roles. The Conservative Party and the business community, traditionally identified with tariff protection and opposition to a free trade agreement, are now the leading advocates. The Liberals, for so long the champions of free trade, oppose the agreement. Even the **Toronto Star,** the largest, most influential publication in Canada, the loudest, most implacable opponent of the agreement, once shouted exactly the same free trade arguments that it now so bitterly attacks.

• In 1911, Conservative leader Robert Laird Borden joined forces with Quebec nationalist leader Henri Bourassa to fight against a free trade deal with the Americans. In 1988, Conservative leader Brian Mulroney has joined forces with Quebec Liberal leader Robert Bourassa to fight for an American free trade deal.

• In 1846, Canada sought and later obtained a limited free trade agreement with the United States, because it was the only way Canadians could see to avoid annexation by the Americans. Today, the fear of being taken over by the United States is the fundamental argument against the free trade agreement.

• The 1854 free trade agreement lasted only 12 years before it was abrogated by the United States. For nearly half a century after that, virtually every major political leader in Canada, from both major parties, unsuccessfully sought another, limited free trade agreement. Finally, when the Americans offered exactly the type of deal that Canada's political leaders had said was needed, Canadian voters turned it down.

• In 1878, the Conservative Party of Sir John A. Macdonald was all set to attack a substantial increase in tariffs expected from the Liberal administration of Alexander Mackenzie. But the Liberals didn't increase the tariff, and the next year, after again winning office, Macdonald brought in the National Policy which established a regime of high tariff protection for the next century.

The National Policy and the Conservatives' platform of "no truck nor trade with the Yankees" three decades later in the 1911 reciprocity election, advocated the use of high protective tariffs for specific purposes. They were intended to avert American domination, assert Canadian independence, arrest massive emigration to the United States, establish a strong manufacturing industry, create jobs and wealth, and establish Canadian nationhood and unity from coast to coast.

How successful the use of protective tariffs and trade restrictions has been in establishing these objectives remains a matter of conjecture and heated debate. After a century of protective trade restrictions, the number of Canadians who have left to reside permanently in the United States exceeds the population of Canada's largest city. After a century of trade protection, no other people in the world are as dependent for jobs on American purchases and American investments as Canadians. No people other than Americans themselves, have invested so much of their savings in the United States. Protection has been attacked by such authorities as the Economic Council of Canada for retarding Canadian employment, investment, technology and our ability to compete with the rest of the world; for diminishing our capacity to act as an independent nation; as a primary cause of regional divisiveness, resentments, and national disunity. A century of protection failed to produce a significant and competitive manufacturing industry. It is only as protection has withered away during the past few years that our ability to compete in the global market has begun to emerge.

How did we get to this state?

It has been a long journey, but the narrative can be greatly compressed into a very brief history.

The first Can-Am free trade agreement

A secret agent armed with bags of money to bribe politicians and newspaper publishers, lavish entertainment, and gunboat diplomacy — including the seizure of 400 American fishing boats — were among the means used to secure the first Canadian-American trade agreement, in 1854.

But long before this, the stage was set by the crusade of liberal economists, social reformers, politicians, and manufacturers who set out to strike from Britain the shackles of protection by the salvation of free trade and the promised grace of prosperity and peace.

"It is as foolish for a nation as for an individual to make what can be bought cheaper," Adam Smith thundered in the Wealth of Nations in 1776, and the preachers of the free trade gospel — men like John Bright and Richard Cobden — echoed the refrain in a rising chorus, with demonstrations and monster rallies throughout England. They were joined by the rapidly expanding British manufacturers who wanted to conquer the world, not with armies and navies but with steel, china, and textiles. The corn laws that imposed duties on imported grains, they argued, kept cheap bread from the working classes and benefited only the landed aristocracy. Low-cost production in English factories was the way to wealth and power, but the way was blocked by the high costs of tariff protection.

The corn laws comforted not only the British aristocracy; they were also an important boon to the farmers, millers, merchants and shippers in the four provinces, or colonies, of pre-confederation British North America — Canada, New Brunswick, Nova Scotia, and Prince Edward Island. The preferential tariffs, with low rates for the colonies and higher duties for everyone else, meant that any British demand for wheat and flour that could not be supplied by the farms of the British aristocracy, was supplied by the farmers and millers of Canada.

Even more important to the BNA provinces were Britain's preferential timber tariffs, established not to protect Britain's land owners (most of the big British oaks had already been felled) but for national security. The Napoleonic wars convinced British leaders that their nation would be vulnerable if they relied on timber from the Baltic countries to keep the British navy afloat. The high tariffs on Baltic wood meant that timber not only for the British navy but also for general construction, came primarily from the provinces of British North America. By the 1840s this import protection cost the British, according to one estimate, £900,000 a year — a terrible burden on Britain but an enormous subsidy for the lumber operations in the provinces.

The most ardent British free traders were no great fans of colonialism. They viewed the defence of far-flung colonies as a burden and a waste; their existence a cause of wars, and a part of the vested interests in maintaining a high level of tariffs. "I wish the British government would give you Canada at once," Lord Ashburton told the American Ambassador John Quincy Adams in 1827. "It is fit for nothing but to breed quarrels."

It was not a liberal economist who ultimately demolished the tariffs and brought free trade to Britain, but a Tory prime minister, Sir Robert Peel, much to the bitter chagrin of his fellow land owners. At the beginning of 1846, Peel announced that the timber tariffs would be slashed, while the corn laws were to be replaced over a period of three years. But because of the great Irish potato famine that killed more than one million people that year, the import duties on grains and flour were completely removed within 12 months.

In the provinces of pre-confederation Canada, the results were seen as the cause of unmitigated disaster.

Nowhere in the provinces did the slash in timber and wheat sales to Britain hit harder than in the business community of Montreal, where for nearly two years bankruptcy was just about the most active business. English speaking people in French Montreal burned with other frustrations. They were burdened with the problems of looking after more than 100,000 refugees who arrived in 1847 from the Irish famine; destitute, disease-ridden, and starving. They blamed England for oppressing these people, then dumping their problem on Canada. They resented legislation to compensate for damages suffered during the abortive rebellion in 1837. And they were deeply concerned that the coming of responsible government would mean the loss of political control to the French-speaking majority of the province. Their frustrations boiled over into a riot that year, in which the Governor General, Lord Elgin, was attacked on the steps of the legislature; the legislature was burned and ransacked, and an angry mob roamed the streets all night, looting and rioting.

In October that year, the Annexation Manifesto was issued in Montreal, demanding both economic and political union with the United States. The petitioners claimed that joining the United States would increase farm prices, lower the cost of imports, achieve greater exports, provide them with a greater voice in the government at Washington than they had in the government at London, and perhaps most importantly would swamp the French in a vast Anglo-Saxon nation. Among the 325 people who signed the Manifesto were John Redpath, the sugar tycoon; the head of Canada's most powerful family, the Molsons; John Rose, later a cabinet minister and head of the Grand Trunk Railway; Alexander Tilloch Galt, who 18 years later would become one of the fathers of confederation; and John Abbott, a future prime minister. It was no mere mob of radicals that saw Canada's best hope in joining the United States.

In Canada West, William Hamilton Merritt, a miller from St. Catharines and the man who had spearheaded construction of the Welland Canal to link Lakes Erie and Ontario for navigation by bypassing the Niagara Falls, had a different vision. In pamphlets and on the platform, in the pages of the **St. Catharines Standard**, and in the legislature where he sat as a reformer (the predecessor of the Liberal party), Hamilton in 1846 became the leading advocate of free trade with the United States as the only possible alternative to annexation.

In 1846, Merritt persuaded the legislature to petition Britain, asking the English to negotiate a free trade treaty with the United States on Canada's behalf. The next year when the province of Canada assumed the responsibility of setting its own tariffs, Merritt persuaded the legislature to lower the duty on imports of American manufactured goods from 12 percent to 7.5 percent, while increasing the duty on British imports from five to seven percent. The legislature adopted an Act offering free trade — or reciprocity — in a list of natural products whenever the Americans were prepared to take similar action. Lobbying in Washington, he succeeded in having a similar bill introduced in the U.S. Congress, but it was defeated in the Senate. Throughout all this, Merritt was in constant communication with the Governor General, Lord Elgin, who wrote to the Colonial office in London that "unless reciprocity with the United States be established, these colonies must be lost to England."

The talks dragged on for eight years, and before they were concluded another factor had entered the equation: a dispute over fishing rights off Nova Scotia and Newfoundland. Nova Scotia claimed that its three-mile territorial limit of exclusive fishing rights extended across all bays, from headland to headland. The Americans claimed that the three-mile limit hugged the shoreline, enabling them to fish inside the larger and wider bays. Partly to force the Americans to come to terms with the demands for a reciprocity treaty, Britain announced that it would send a naval force to protect the fisheries. The United States replied by sending a warship to protect its fishermen. Confrontation on the high seas was avoided — at least for a time — when Britain and the United States agreed to negotiate a treaty to settle both the fisheries dispute and trade with the BNA provinces. The elegant Elgin was sent to Washington as a special envoy to negotiate the treaty.

A pathway through the political undergrowth had already been hacked away by special agent Israel de Wolfe Andrews. A native of Eastport, Maine, Andrews had started his working career facilitating North American trade by engaging in the popular business of smuggling. Some historians would have us believe that by working throughout the night at this covert business, Andrews became a life-long advocate of free trade. He certainly became a fast talker. In 1849 he persuaded the American Secretary of State to assign him on a secret mission to gather statistical information and other data concerning the trade of the four BNA provinces. Then he persuaded the British Ambassador in Washington to give him a similar assignment., while still secretly working for the Americans. In early 1853, after conferring with President Pierce and Secretary of State Marcy, Andrews was appointed "special agent" of the United States Government to cultivate support in both the United States and the provinces for approval of a reciprocity agreement. Next he persuaded the City of Boston and the Government of Canada to provide further funds for the same cause. With offices in the Astor House in New York and the National Hotel in Washington, Andrews spent more than a year as an early-day lobbyist and public relations hit man, entertaining politicians and newspapermen on both sides of the border, writing pamphlets, arranging supportive editorials, and placing funds with influential people. He collected $110,000 from his sponsors for this work — an enormous sum in 1854 — but claimed to have spent more than $200,000. He spent the rest of his life seeking to collect the extra $90,000, but had difficulty substantiating his claims because of the secret nature of his work and the supposed embarrassment that would result by revealing with whom the money had been placed. Unable to pay his debts, Andrews spent several short periods in jail, and died a destitute alcoholic.

With the early advocacy by Merritt, with gunboat diplomacy, with the lobbying of Andrews, with Lord Elgin's charm, wit and gracious entertaining, the Reciprocity Act of 1854 was, as Elgin's secretary noted, "floated through on champagne." The agreement provided for free trade in such natural products as farm produce, fish, timber, coal, and other minerals. Americans were allowed to fish in the disputed waters off Nova Scotia and Newfoundland, to use the Canadian shores to dry their fish, and Canadian ports for provisioning. The Maritimers, in turn, could fish off the American coast as far south as North Carolina, but more importantly, they had free access to the big American market. It was not, however, the last time that the fisheries became embroiled in dispute, or used as bait in trade talks.

Abrogation, confederation, and the National Policy (1854-1891)

During the 12 years that it remained in effect, until March 1866, the reciprocity treaty brought good times to the four BNA provinces, as the value of trade with the United States tripled. How much of the prosperity was due to the free trade and how much was due to other factors is still a subject of debate by economic historians, but for Canadians of that era there was no doubt that free trade with the Americans was a very good thing.

With the end of the American civil war, however, the end of the treaty was also in sight. The Americans, as required under the terms of the treaty, gave a little more than one year's notice before the treaty was terminated. There were a number of causes: growing protectionist sentiment in the northern United States; American resentment of British sympathy for the south during the war; American resentment of some small-scale raids against the United States that had been launched by Confederate forces from Canada; a hope by some that abrogating the treaty might lead to annexation of Canada in the American drive for manifest destiny. It did not help that the anti-Americanism that has grown like a cancer into the bones of so much of Canada's nationalism, had already begun to germinate. Sniffed Lord Minto, a later Governor General: "There is a general dislike of the Yankees here and I do not wonder at it... What the Canadian sees and hears is constant Yankee bluff and swagger & that eventually he means to possess Canada for himself."

The provinces hoped that the treaty would be extended, but they prepared for its end, planning to create their own free market among themselves, and then hopefully some day extend and expand it westward. Canada was planned as the response to the end of free trade with the Americans. A delegation from the provinces to a colonial conference in London reported that they had "explained the immediate injury that would result to Canadian interests from the abrogation of the Treaty; but we pointed out at the same time the new and ultimately more profitable channels into which our foreign trade must, in that event, be turned, and the necessity of preparing for change, if indeed it was to come." Nine months after the Americans had given their notice, the provinces formed a Confederate Council of Trade, with two objectives: to form an economic union among themselves, and to re-establish trade reciprocity with the United States.

Confederation did not bring the quest for a free trade agreement with the United States, or reciprocity, to an end. The first tariff established by Canada the year after confederation offered to eliminate import duties on specified imports from the United States whenever the Americans were prepared to reciprocate.

The long procession of formal and informal missions to Washington to seek a renewed reciprocity agreement, started almost immediately. John Rose, the first Conservative minister of finance, led the parade in 1869, followed two years later by John A. Macdonald himself. The Liberal administration of Alexander Mackenzie in 1874 sent George Brown, who actually obtained the support of President Grant for a draft agreement providing for free trade in 60 specified natural products, agricultural implements, and 37 other categories of manufactured goods. But the American Congress refused to even consider it. The Conservatives sent yet another emissary, Charles

Tupper, in 1887; Macdonald made his last pitch to the Americans in 1892, and Wilfrid Laurier made the final pilgrimage in 1896.

Not even the fisheries bait and gunboat diplomacy could budge the Americans into another reciprocity agreement. When the first treaty had been abrogated in 1866, Americans lost the right to fish in disputed Canadian waters, and Britain and Canada several times tried to use this as a bargaining chip. In 1870, Canada seized 400 American fishing boats, much to the wrath of the Americans. It was to settle both this and secure a trade treaty that Macdonald had accompanied British officials to Washington the following year. He returned without the trade treaty, and with the fisheries dispute only temporarily resolved.

In between all these negotiations, Macdonald established the National Policy, which was claimed to have a double purpose. On the one hand, it set high tariffs to encourage the establishment of factories and manufacturing in Canada. On the other hand, the high tariffs were said to be a tool, which would pry a reciprocity agreement from the Americans. "Why should they give us reciprocity when they have our markets open to them now?" was Macdonald's rhetorical question in Parliamentary debate. "It is only by closing our doors and cutting them out of our markets that they will open theirs to us." The National Policy would establish both free trade and protectionism, at the same time.

Some said the reason the Conservatives had adopted a protective tariff policy was because the Liberals had not. It was 1876. The Liberal administration of Alexander Mackenzie had been in power nearly four years, and would soon have to face the voters. It was Mackenzie's luck to win office just at the start of the first Great Depression, a quarter of a century of gloom interrupted by only a few brief periods of economic sunshine. Tough times sharpened the trade debate. Manufacturers clamored for protection. The staples producers — farmers, fishermen, lumbermen, miners — demanded commercial union with the United States. The country's population was shrinking as Canadians, especially from Quebec, flocked to the United States.

In the Liberal camp, the free trade champion was Richard Cartwright, best remembered, said one historian, for his "improbable whiskers and uniquely passionate hatred of John A. Macdonald." The scion of a wealthy loyalist family, Cartwright had substantial business interests in transportation, mining, real estate, manufacturing, and had started political life as a Conservative, until he quarreled with Macdonald. Minister of finance in Mackenzie's administration, Cartwright had hectored so vociferously for free trade that the Conservatives called him the Blue Ruin Knight. The advantages of free trade with the United States were so great,

Cartwright declared "that scarcely any sacrifice is too great to secure them." It was not free trade but the lack of free trade that threatened to drive Canada into the arms of the United States, according to Cartwright. As for any loyalty or obligation owed to Britain, Cartwright argued that because of how the British had botched negotiations with the Americans, all that was owed was Christian forgiveness.

> ## John A. Macdonald may have died a British subject, but he was buried in an American casket.

The hard times also hit government revenues, which, before income tax was invented, depended primarily on the tariff. The Liberal budget in 1873 was expected to bring a much higher tariff. Conservative finance critic Charles Tupper had reportedly prepared his speech for the House, attacking the anticipated high tariffs. When they failed to appear, Tupper asked that the House rise early, and later that evening delivered his speech, attacking the Liberals for failing to provide protection. The story was later elaborated by one of the leaders in the Conservative caucus, Dalton McCarthy:

> No doubt in the world the Conservative party were put out of power [in 1873] and by going in for the National Policy and taking the wind out of Mr. Mackenzie's sales, we got into power. We became identified with the protective policy, and if Mr. Mackenzie had adopted a protective policy, we would have been free traders. I am willing to make this confession, that if Mr. Mackenzie had been a protectionist there would have been nothing left but for us to be free traders. But Mr. Mackenzie was either too honest or too earnest in his opinions to bend to the wave of public opinion and the result was that he was swept out of power and had only a corporal's guard to support him when the House met.

Beyond doubt the Conservatives were swept back into power on the National Policy platform when the election came in 1878, but there's little conclusive evidence that it attained its stated objectives. The National Policy established an average import duty of 28 percent: 25 percent on agricultural implements, 30 percent on railway equipment, 25 percent on woolen clothing; 30 percent plus half a cent a pound on refined sugar. But it did nothing to slow the exodus of Canadians leaving to live in the United States. The year after the policy was established, the number of Canadians emigrating to the

United States increased 300 percent, while the following year it increased a further 25 percent. In the two decades after the policy was established, some 1.5 million people immigrated to Canada — and two million left.

Organized labor was just starting to emerge in Canada, and the attitude of the labor leaders was reflected in the **Labor Advocate,** the journal of the Toronto Trades and Labor Council. Building Canada as a separate nation, said the **Advocate,** was "the greatest and most stupendous blunder," for which "the CPR was built, the protective tariff created, the northwest land monopolies endorsed, and the people's money squandered in immigration."

The free trade debate dominated the next election, too, in 1891. Wilfrid Laurier had now assumed the leadership of the Liberals, and for their campaign platform they had adopted a policy of "unrestricted reciprocity" — complete free trade with the United States in both natural products and manufactured goods. Macdonald sought to steal the Liberal platform by arguing that the Conservatives could use high tariffs to compel the Americans to agree to reciprocity, and that the Americans had, in fact, already suggested such an arrangement. But when American Secretary of State John Blaine wrote that "There are no negotiations whatever on foot for a reciprocity treaty with Canada, and you may be assured that no such scheme for reciprocity with the Dominion confined to natural products will be entertained by this government," Macdonald quickly shifted ground. He now attacked reciprocity as a scheme designed to break up the British Empire.

"A British subject I was born, a British subject I will die," Macdonald declared. "With my utmost effort, with my latest breath, I will oppose the 'veiled treason' which attempts by sordid means and mercenary proffers to lure our people from their allegiance." The Tories rolled out their banner — "the old flag, the old man, and the old party" — and won the election. Three months later, Macdonald had died.

Macdonald may have died a British subject, but he was buried in a casket made in West Meriden, Connecticut, described as "an exact facsimile of that of the late President Garfield." It was symbolic of the National Policy, which ultimately could not overcome the pull of geography, economics, and common sense.

Wilfrid Laurier led his party to victory in 1896, and the Liberals were soon accused of preaching free trade in opposition and practicing protectionism in power. Goldwyn Smith, the intellectual gad-fly who preached not just economic union but political union with the United States, has described how the Liberals supposedly sold out to the manufacturers at meetings held in the "Red Parlour" of the Queen's Hotel in Toronto: "...on the neck of the Canadians... now rides an association of protected manufacturers making the community and all the great interests of the country tributary to their aims. Before a general election, the Prime Minister calls these men together in the parlour of a Toronto hotel, receives their contributions to his election fund, and pledges the commercial policy of the country."

A harsh judgement. But in fact, given the political need to reconcile conflicting demands, Laurier probably went as far as he could to liberalize the tariff — even if that was not a great distance. He renewed the quest for a reciprocal treaty with the United States, and when he was rebuffed declared, "There will be no more pilgrimages to Washington. We are turning our hopes to the old motherland." In its first two years, the Laurier administration eliminated the tariff on imported binder twine, reduced it on agricultural implements and refined sugar, arranged a preferential tariff that reduced the cost of British imports, and subsequently made other small adjustments.

The 16 years of the Laurier administration brought unprecedented expansion and prosperity. The depression that had hung so long over North America and Europe had at last lifted. Seventy million acres of farm land were settled in the west. People poured in to fill up this empty country: 784,000 from the United States; 961,000 from Britain; 594,000 from other parts of Europe. Laurier seemed right when he said the 20th century belonged to Canada.

How the Laurier era was ended by the great reciprocity election of 1911 has been told too often to bear repeating in detail. Perhaps more than ever before the country was pulled by the conflicting demands of protection and free trade. On a tour of the west in 1910, Laurier was met at massive meetings by tens of thousands of farmers who were angry at being squeezed by high, tariff-supported prices for everything they bought, and low-prices for everything they sold, pushed down by world markets and the cost of railway transportation. "In 1896 you promised to skin the Tory bear of protection," a farmer in Saskatoon bellowed. "Have you done it? If so, I would like to ask what you've done with the hide." But in Vancouver, Laurier met a delegation of lumber interests who demanded protection. And W.H. Rowley, president of the Canadian Manufacturers Association, told the association's 1910 annual meeting:

> In season and out of season, in favor and out of favor, liked or disliked, I have always believed in protection, have always advocated it, and will always continue to do so. I have no politics other than protection, and I hope none of you have. If you have them, I think you should sink them for the good of the Association, for protection is the only politics the Association should recognize.

In Washington, President Taft saw some potential political

advantage in reciprocity, which could lower food costs for consumers and newsprint costs for newspaper publishers. Through the editor of the **Toronto Globe,** Taft made it known that he would like to talk trade, and in a series of meetings finance minister W.S. Fielding and the Americans hammered out the terms of an agreement. When Fielding outlined those terms in the House on January 26, the Tories were stunned by the range of products that would gain duty-free entry into the huge U.S. market. The Liberals, reported the Montreal Herald, "cheered and cheered again." Even some Conservative members from the west could not resist cheering. During the next couple of days, Conservative newspapers were among those that approved the agreement.

But the railways and manufacturers quickly rallied the opposition. "Bust the damn thing," CPR president William Van Horn ordered. The opposition was strengthened by 18 prominent Liberal businessmen — led by Laurier's former cabinet strongman, Clifford Sifton — who came out strongly against reciprocity.

Conservative leader Robert Borden forged two alliances to fight the election. In Quebec, he joined forces with Henri Bourassa, leader of the Nationalists, in an appeal to anti-British sentiment. In Ontario he was joined by the railways and manufacturers in an emotional appeal to pro-British and anti-American sentiment. Borden met in Toronto with four of the leading Liberal defectors — Sifton; Z.A. Lash, from Canadian Northern Railways; Lloyd Harris, who represented the Massey-Harris interests; J.S. Willison, editor of the **Toronto News.** The Liberals outlined the terms for their support. Quebec and Roman Catholics were not to have an undue influence in any future Conservative government; Borden would bring men from outside Parliament into his cabinet; in forming a cabinet, Borden would consult with Lash, Willison, and Sir Edmund Walker, president of the Bank of Commerce. Borden agreed. By mid-August, some 9.5 million pieces of anti-reciprocity literature had been published by the Canadian National League, the Canadian Manufacturers Association, and the Canadian Home Market Association. The tone is indicated by the title of one tract," An Appeal to the British-born." On election day it was Conservatives 134 seats, Liberals 87.

Historian Edgar McInnis has summed up the election this way: "After long years of alternate bullying at the hands of their stronger neighbors, Canadians seized on an opportunity to assert their independence of spirit, and, under an emotional upsurge that had nothing to do with logic, they rebuffed the United States by rejecting an agreement that Canada had been seeking for the past 70 years."

The vote, however, was much closer than the standings: 666,074 for the Conservatives, 623,554 for the Liberals. Farmers had voted for reciprocity, and in Alberta and Saskatchewan the Liberals had won 15 of 17 seats. From the bitter disappointment of the farmers emerged the Progressive Party, which campaigned in 1921 under the free trade banner to eclipse the Tories for second position in the House, with 65 seats to 50. The Liberals, under Mackenzie King, held 117 seats and a Parliamentary majority of one. The national policy prevailed, but the spirit of free trade survived.

King, Bennett, depression, war, and a secret agreement

As he clasped the fragile key to office, the free trade flame may well have continued to flicker in the heart of William Lyon Mackenzie King, but he would never forget that it was this cause that 10 years earlier had cost him his Parliamentary seat as the boyish face on Laurier's team. Doing anything about his preference for a lower tariff was not made any easier by U.S. action the same year that Mackenzie King returned the Liberals to power. The Americans raised their tariff wall a little higher with the 1921 Emergency Tariff Act, and Canadian sales to the United States that year fell by more than 40 percent.

In early 1930, at the outset of the Great Depression, U.S. duties jumped 50 percent with the Smoot-Hawley Act. King retaliated by increasing Canadian duties on American imports, and lowering them on British imports. American tariffs now averaged an astounding 37 percent; Canada's tariffs, 26 percent. In October, Richard Bedford Bennett rode in from Calgary to take over as prime minister, promising to use his tariff guns to "blast the way to world markets." The tariff got higher — reaching 30 percent in 1933 — and the depression got worse. Nowhere was it as bad as on the prairies. From 1928 to 1933, per capita income across Canada fell by an average of nearly 50 percent; in Alberta, by 60 percent; in Saskatchewan by 72 percent, according to one estimate. The tariff was blamed for skewering Atlantic and Western Canada. In 1934, the Government of Nova Scotia estimated that the tariff amounted to an annual subsidy of $15.15 for everyone in Ontario and $11.03 for everyone in Quebec, subsidies paid for by other Canadians at rates varying from $11.67 per person in Nova Scotia to $28.16 in Saskatchewan. In the 1930s, you could eat for two months for less than $30 — and many were hungry. More than a quarter of a million people left the prairies, and abandoned farms dotted the skyline.

Bennett and President Roosevelt met in 1933 and at last agreed "to begin a search for means to increase the exchange of commodities between our two countries." But progress was very slow, until King was again returned to power in 1935, and set his trade officials to work at a "terrific pace" to work out a trade treaty with the Americans. By November, agreement had been reached on the first Canadian-

American trade treaty in nearly a century. It was not free trade, but it did slash the tariffs, and it accomplished what it was supposed to. In the next two years, Canadian-American trade increased by more than 50 percent.

Negotiations began on even further cuts, but this time they also involved reducing the tariff preference on British imports, thus requiring complex three-way negotiations. "Our discussions with the U.S. are the least of our worries right now," wrote Norman Robertson, a senior official in the Department of External Affairs. "We can cope with them but not with God's Englishmen and the inescapable moral ascendancy over us lesser breeds." But agreement was reached with God's Englishmen, as well as with the Americans, and tariffs were reduced still more. By the time the Second World War arrived in 1939, the back of the depression had been broken — if not by free trade, at least by freer trade.

Canadian-American trade did not become a big issue again until 1947, when a free trade agreement was secretly pursued as the solution to a severe dollar crisis. The world by then had resolved that never again would protectionism lead to such massive misery and destruction, and Canada was one of the nations leading the way to peace and prosperity through the General Agreement on Tariffs and Trade. But now Canada faced a crisis that could cause it to restrict imports, at least temporarily. After the war, Canada had loaned Britain and other European nations some $2 billion — 15 percent of Canada's gross national product — to help European recovery, in return counting on these nations to buy Canadian goods and help create Canadian jobs. But the devastated European nations could not pay cash for Canadian food and supplies. Meanwhile, Canadians were spending $2 for American goods and services for every $1 sold to the Americans.

Something would have to be done. Like a debtor that can't pay its bills on time, Canada approached its creditor, the Americans, to see if something could be worked out. Among the parade of officials who left Ottawa to talk things over with the Americans in Washington were Hector McKinnon, chairman of the Canadian Tariff Board, and John Deutsch, a senior official with the Department of Finance. It was McKinnon and Deutsch who had just recently negotiated Canada's participation in GATT. An American memorandum on the first informal meeting held in Washington by McKinnon and Deutsch said the two Canadians felt that "Canada must either integrate her economy more closely with that of the United States, or be forced into discriminatory restrictive policies" with a "danger of friction with the United States, if not economic war."

Deutsch, the son of a Saskatchewan farmer, was a born-in-the-bones free trader. In a confidential letter to a newspaper friend,

Deutsch wrote: "We have the choice between two kinds of worlds — a relatively free enterprise world with the highest existing standard of living, and a government-controlled world with a lower standard of living." If the answer seemed obvious, Deutsch also warned that the first choice "means meshing our economy as much as possible with that of the United States."

After several weeks of informal talks, the Americans approached Deutsch "on a strictly confidential and private basis" at a New Year's eve dinner party in Washington. A conventional customs union was politically out of the question, since that would, in effect, allow the Americans to dictate Canada's tariff with the rest of the world. The Americans suggested a modified customs union in which there would be substantially free trade between the two countries, but each would set its own tariffs on trade with other nations.

In Ottawa, there was strong support for the idea by Trade Minister C.D. Howe, Finance Minister Douglas Abbott, and even Mackenzie King. McKinnon and Deutsch were authorized to work out the details of an agreement with the Americans, which they did.

On April 1, 1948 Deutsch met with Abbott, Howe, Louis St. Laurent (who would be prime minister when King retired within a few months), and Lester Pearson (then under secretary of state for external affairs). Howe, Pearson and King were all in favor. Howe thought it would make a magnificent issue for the Liberals in the next election. Abbott and St. Laurent expressed concern about the short length of time to secure Congressional approval for a treaty before the U.S. presidential election in November.

The decision turned on King, but his initial ardor had already cooled. An editorial in **Life Magazine** two weeks before this meeting, calling for a conventional type of customs union between Canada and the United States, did not help. It sounded a bit too much like the Americans whose unthinking out loud had helped lead to the still-remembered reciprocity defeat in 1911, like Congressman Champ Clark who had said, "I am for it because I hope to see the day when the American flag will float over every square foot of British North American possessions, clear to the North Pole."

Later in a letter to Norman Robertson, then High Commissioner in London, Pearson described how the decision had been taken at the April fool's day meeting. King, wrote Pearson, had agreed that "from the economic point of view, there was everything to be said for the proposal and little against it." But on political grounds, King felt that "the Conservatives would seize on this issue... in order to force an early election. They would distort and misrepresent the proposal as an effort on the part of the Liberals to sell Canada to the United States for a mess of pottage. All the old British flag-waving would be resurrected by the Conservatives." The others apparently did not share this concern, but they acquiesced to King's decision, although they "felt particular regret at the necessity of coming to this conclusion."

Ottawa was forced to impose temporary restrictions on how much Canadians could spend on American goods and travel (no more than $150 a year for pleasure travel in the U.S.), but the dollar crisis passed, helped by large American investments, by the 1947 discovery of oil in Alberta, and other economic developments. John Deutsch was reportedly bitter about the loss of this opportunity,. but in the end he was proven right. The tariff continued to shrink, the Canadian economy became more closely integrated with that of the United States, and by comparison with virtually any other era or area, prosperity was unprecedented.

The question for every Canadian

There is one question that every Canadian must decide: whether or not to join the United States. It is a question that has always faced Canadians, and always will. It is a question that is decided either by conscious, deliberate choice, or unconsciously, without the slightest consideration. Those who decide to join the United States, do so by simply moving a few miles south, to look for better jobs, or bigger opportunities, or perhaps just a warmer climate. It is a choice that has so far been made by some four million who have left Canada to take up permanent residence in the United States. For many Canadians, deciding not to join the United States has been made a much more difficult choice because of the effects of a century of trade protection.

There are probably now more people living in the United States who moved there from Canada, or are descendents of former Canadians, than in our four western provinces.

The flood of Canadians heading south has been greatest in periods when times have been toughest and trade restrictions greatest; especially during the last decades of the 19th century and during the 1930s. We now face resurgent pressure for protection, and concern about the possibility of another recession.

Would rejection of the free trade agreement this time lead to another mass emigration of Canadians, perhaps even to the breakup of Canada, led by the west? That fear has been expressed. This much seems certain: the free trade agreement will make it easier to decide not to join the United States. And no Canadian can avoid a decision.

Bibliography

Books

Barthe, Ulric. *Sir Wilfrid Laurier on the Platform, 1871-1890*. Montreal, 1890.

Brebner, John B. *North Atlantic Triangle.* New York: Columbia University Press, 1945.

Brown, Craig. *Canada's National Policy, 1883-1900.*.Princeton: Princeton University Press, 1964.

Brown, Craig, and Cook, Ramsay. *Canada 1896-1921: A Nation Transformed.* Toronto: Macmillan, 1974.

Borden, Henry. *Robert Laird Borden: His Memoirs (two volumes).* Toronto: Macmillan, 1938. Reprinted by McClelland and Stewart, 1969.

Duncan, Cameron (editor). *The Free Trade Papers.* Toronto:James Lorimer & Company, 1986.

Careless, J.M.S. *The Union of the Canadas.* Toronto: McClelland and Stewart, 1967.

Creighton, Donald. *John A. Macdonald: The Young Politician.* Toronto: Macmillan, 1952.

_____. *John A. Macdonald: the Old Chieftain.* Toronto: Macmillan, 1955.

Cross, Michael (editor). *Free trade, annexation and reciprocity, 1846-1854.* Holt, Rinehart & Winston, 1971.

Dales, J.H. *The protective tariff in Canada's development.* Toronto: University of Toronto Press, 1966.

Easterbrook, W.T., and Aitken, Hugh, G.H. *Canadian Economic History.* Toronto: Gage Publishing Limited, 1980.

Gwyn,Richard. *The 49th Paradox.*. Toronto: McClelland and Stewart, 1985.

Leacy, F.H. (editor). Historical Statistics of Canada, Second Series. Ottawa: Statistics Canada, 1982

Masters, Donald C. *The Reciprocity Treaty of 1854.* Longman's Green and Company, 1937. Reprinted by McClelland and Stewart, 1963.

Merritt, William Hamilton. *Letters Addressed to the Inhabitants of the Niagara District on Free Trade and Commerce.* Niagara: John Simpson, 1847.

_____. *Remarks on the Extension of Reciprocity between Canada and the United States.* St. Catharines: H. Leavenworth, 1855.

McInnis, Edgar. *Canada: A Political and Social History.* New York: Rinehart & Winston, 1961.

Naylor, Tom *The History of Canadian Business.* Toronto: James Lorimer & Company, 1975.

Porritt, Edward. *The revolt in Canada against the new feudalism.* London: Cassells & Co., 1911.

_____.. *Sixty years of protection in Canada.* Winnipeg: Grain Growers Guide, 1913.

Schull, Joseph. *Laurier: The first Canadian.* Toronto: Macmillan, 1965.

Shippee, L.B. *Canadian-American relations, 1849-74.* New Haven: Yale University Press,1939.

Waite, P.B. *Life and Times of Confederation: 1864-1867.* Toronto: University of Toronto Press, 1962.

Skelton, Oscar Douglas. *Life and Letters of Sir Wilfrid Laurier (two volumes).* Toronto: McClelland and Stewart, 1971.

Stevens, Paul (editor). *The 1911 general election: a study in Canadian politics.* Toronto: Copp Clark, 1970

United States, Department of Commerce, Bureau of Statistics. *Historical Statistics of the United States, Colonial Times to 1970.* Washington, 1975.

Other sources

Argyle, Ray. *The federal election of September 21, 1911.* Unpublished manuscript, Toronto, nd.

Baker, W.M. A case study of Anti-Americanism in English-Speaking Canada: The Election Campaign of 1911. *Canadian Historical Review,* December, 1970.

Craven, Paul, and Traves, Tom. The class politics of the National Policy, 1872-1933. *Journal of Canadian Studies,* Fall, 1979.

Cuff, Robert. The Conservative Party Machine and the Election of 1911. *Ontario History, September, 1965.*

—————. The Toronto eighteen and the election of 1911. *Ontario History,* December, 1963.

Cuff, Robert, and Granatstein, J.L. The rise and fall of Canadian-American free trade. *Canadian Historical Review,* December, 1977.

Deutsch, John. Private papers. Archives, Queen's University, Kingston.

—————. Papers. Public Archives of Canada. Department of Finance Records (RG-19), Vol. 3606. Memorandum, "Pattern and Future Development of Canadian External Trade." 1946. (nd,na).

Graham, W.R. Sir Richard Cartwright, Wilfrid Laurier and Liberal Party Trade Policy, 1887. *Canadian Historical Review,* March, 1952.

Granatstein, J.L. Free trade between Canada and the United States, the issue that will not go away. In volume 29 of the *Report of the Royal Commission on the Economic Union and Development Prospects for Canada,* Ottawa, 1985.

Forster, Benjamin. The coming of the national policy: business, government and the tariff, 1876-1879. *Journal of Canadian Studies.* Fall, 1979.

Hecht, Irene W.D. Israel D. Andrews and the Reciprocity Treaty of 1854: A Reappraisal. *Canadian Historical Review,* December, 1963.

MacKirdy, K.A. The loyalty issue in the 1891 federal election campaign, and an ironic footnote. *Ontario History.* September, 1963.

Masters, Donald C. A further word on I.D. Andrews and the Reciprocity Treaty of 1854. Canadian Historical Review, June, 1936.

Mirror of Parliament. Province of Canada, Second Session, Second Parliament. (Statement by W.H. Merritt in House of Assembly, June 1, 1846). Montreal, 1846.

Overman, William D. *I.D. Andrews and Reciprocity in 1854.* Canadian Historical Review, September, 1934.

Phillips, Paul. The National Policy Revisited. *Journal of Canadian Studies,* Fall, 1979.

Watt, F.W. The National Policy, the Working Man, and Proletarian Ideas in Victorian Canada. *Canadian Historical Review, 1959.*

Wilson, George. A note on Israel Dewolfe Andrews: Opportunist or Diplomat? *Canadian Historical Review,* September, 1969.

Chapter two:
From Adam Smith to Donald Macdonald

The obstacles to free trade

Adam Smith, from An Inquiry into the Nature and Causes of The Wealth of Nations., Glasgow, 1776.

To expect, indeed, that freedom of trade should ever be entirely restored in Great Britain, is as absurd as to expect that an Oceana or Utopia should ever be established in it. Not only the prejudices of the public, but what is much more unconquerable, the private interest of many individuals, irresistibly oppose it. Were the officers of the army to oppose with the same zeal and unanimity any reduction in the number of forces, with which master manufacturers set themselves against every law that is likely to increase the number of their rivals in the home market; were the former to animate their soldiers, in the same manner as the latter enflame their workmen, to attack with violence and outrage the proposers of any such regulation; to attempt to reduce the army would be as dangerous as it has now become to attempt to diminish in any respect the monopoly which our manufacturers have obtained against us. This monopoly has so much increased the number of some particular tribes of them, that, like an overgrown standing army, they have become formidable to the government, and upon many occasions intimidate the legislature.

Free trade or annexation

William Hamilton Merritt. Excerpts from remarks in moving resolutions in the Legislature of Canada proposing trade reciprocity with the United States. Quoted in The St. Catharines Journal, May 14, 1846.

Examine the Journals of Upper Canada during that period [1835-1837]: you will find there the efforts then made to obtain access to the market of the United States. A petition numerously signed was forwarded to Congress praying for admission of their products. The state of the markets, no doubt, was one of the ruling causes which led the inhabitants of Upper Canada to open revolt, and a resort to arms in 1837.

If no remedy is provided the same cause will again exist in 1849 [when all British duties on grain imports were scheduled to be removed: they were actually removed in 1846]. Let us now apply our minds to the application of a remedy.

Sir Robert Peel very justly observes that high duties, called protection, is a false reliance, a delusion on the part of the laborer, and a clear loss to the revenue, both are robbed by the smuggler. Houses in Paris will guarantee the delivery of goods in London for 15 per cent. If with their numerous excise, coast guards and cruisers, goods can be smuggled there at 15 per cent they can here for one half, or 7-1/2 percent. No person can be induced to embark capital in manufactures in Canada, under the expectation that any duty, however high it may appear, will protect him from competition in the same article from the United States....

It is evident, Mr. Speaker, that if protection be withdrawn in the markets of Britain it is impractical in Canada: we have no means of enforcing it; we are powerless....

... Also, That Her Majesty may be pleased to open a negotiation with the Government of the United States for the purpose of obtaining access for the products of Canada into the markets of that country on the same terms that American products are to be admitted into the markets of Britain and Canada....

I am sensible, Mr. Speaker, that many men of sound judgment entertain the opinion that if a free intercourse were opened with the United States, on the same terms as between the citizens of different States, that it would lead to a separation from the mother country — this opinion was expressed in the address of the North American Colonial Association in January last. They apprehend a change in the sentiments of the colonists, if no preference in the markets of the mother country, in case they are offered a free interchange of commodities with the United States. I entertain the very opposite opinion. A change in the sentiments of the colonists can only arise in their being deprived of this free intercourse... I will assign but one reason, a farmer values his market by comparative not remunerative prices — if equal on both sides of the boundary, and wheat came down to 2s 6d., he would rest satisfied, but not if he received 4s 4d and the American farmer 4s 6d per bushel. This inequality may not lead to the same result as in 1837, but it will produce a strong inclination to form a part of the United States. On the contrary, were our products admitted into their markets, no difference in prices would be visible; the Canadian farmer at all times would be placed on an equal footing, in all respects, with the Western farmer. This is all the favor he asks; and so far from feeling any desire to change his political institutions, he would realize the advantages he possessed and resist any political change.

Why limit it to natural products?

William Hamilton Merritt. Excerpts from Remarks on the Extension of Reciprocity between Canada and the United States (now confined to the Growth and Produce of Each) to Manufacturing, Shipping & Coasting, and Establishing a Commercial System adapted to the Geographical Position of Canada. St. Catharines, 1855.

The advantages to arise from the introduction of this principle are obvious.

Capital will be introduced and expended in the erection of Manufactories — a population now idle will find profitable employment during the long winter season, without diverting the industry of a single man from Agriculture — our extensive water power, now useless, will be converted into a source of wealth; and our lakes, rivers, canals and railways, now unproductive, will transport the raw material and manufactured articles, at the lowest prices, from or to any portion of the Continent, at a profit. With these facilities, and every material for building, bread and every description of provisions at the cheapest rates, no reason can be assigned, when placed on the same footing, why Canada should not manufacture the like article as cheap and extensive as any other portion of America....

In place of from one-eighth to one-fifth of our industry being lost, in the exchange of our productions, the grower will receive the highest prices for every article he sells, and the consumer will be furnished, at the lowest prices, with every article that he purchases, and the profits will be added to the general wealth of both countries. In short, every individual who gains a living by labor, is personally interested in the early adoption of this principle....

But we may look for an active opposition from among ourselves. It is the general impression, that reciprocity between the United States and Canada will lead not only to the removal of duties on the particular article produced, but to the removal of every Customs establishment in the interior... Individuals who may compose the Government for the time being, will be unwilling voluntarily to surrender that patronage by which they retain power; neither will individuals who are dependant for their subsistence on the salaries and perquisites they receive, be willing to give them up — while the public feel very little, if any, personal interest in the question; and I am constrained to admit, that we have not yet a sufficient growth of Canadian feeling to advocate any measure with no other motive than promoting the interest of Canada.

The Report of the Committee [of the Legislature of Canada] advocates no protection: no public bounty — no temporary aid to build up any separate interest. Its object is the removal of all Legislative restrictions on Trade.

This accursed tariff

Thomas Watson, Commissioner of Public Works for Manitoba, and later a Liberal Senator. At a national Liberal convention, Ottawa, June 21, 1893.

We in the west have even a greater disadvantage than that of the railway freights in this accursed tariff, which has borne so heavily on the settler. I am free to admit that with us many of the people are hard up. How could it be otherwise under such a system? I have no hesitation in saying that if the money unjustly taken from the pockets of the people were returned, every man would be able to pay off his debts and have something to his credit in the bank. We have no use for protection in the Northwest, for nothing is raised in price for the benefit of the farmer, but on everything he buys he has to pay extra on account of the tariff. Therefore, we want the freest trade possible... What the people of Manitoba want is a free field and no favor. As it is now we are compelled to sell our produce in the markets of the world, and then we have to turn around and buy our supplies in a protected market.

Tariff bondage, as in slavery

Wilfrid Laurier, Winnipeg, September 2, 1894.

We stand for freedom. I denounce the policy of protection as bondage — yea, bondage; and I refer to bondage in the same manner in which American slavery was bondage. Not in the same degree, perhaps, but in the same manner. In the same manner the people of Canada, the inhabitants of the City of Winnipeg especially, are toiling for a master who takes away not every cent of profit but a very large percentage, a very large portion of your earnings for which you sweat and toil.

When the regulators and regulated get together

Dalton McCarthy, Conservative Member of Parliament, April 11, 1894.

There is not a manufacturing industry in this country in which there is not an understanding between the men engaged in it by which they regulate the output and fix the prices, and there is virtually no competition. What is the result? The result is that you are paying an enormous tax on what you bring into the country, that goes into the Treasury. The duty that your merchant pays to the customs house officers goes into the Treasury. He adds it to the price of his goods, his profit to that, and it comes out of the pockets of the people. But if you deal with the home manufacturer you pay him the same price as if he had paid the duty, when he has not paid anything, and the 35 percent goes into his pocket and not into the Treasury at all.

A form of state socialism

Thomas F. Bayard, United States Minister in London, 1893-1897, at Edinborough, November 7, 1895.

In my own country I have witnessed the insatiable growth of that form of state socialism styled protection, which I believe has done more than any other single cause to foster class legislation and create inequality of fortune, to corrupt public life, to banish men of independent mind and character from the public councils, to lower the tone of national representation, blunt public conscience, create false standards in the popular mind, to familiarise it with reliance on state aid and guardianship in private affairs, divorce ethics from politics, and place politics upon the low level of a mercenary scramble.

Farmers want to sell for more and buy for less

J.W. Scanlon, Honorary President, Manitoba Grain Growers Association, in a petition delivered at a meet with Prime Minister Wilfrid Laurier, Brandon, June 18, 1907.

There are no trade arrangements the Canadian Government could make with any country that would meet with greater favour or stronger support from the farmers of Western Canada than a wide measure of reciprocal trade with the United States, including manufactured articles and the natural product of both countries. Such a trade arrangement would give the Canadian farmers, especially the Western farmers, a larger and better market in which to sell and a cheaper market in which to buy... The farmers know that a lowering of our tariff or freer trade with the United States will be strongly opposed by the united strength of the protected interests which have developed such strength and grown to such power and wealth under our protective tariff and because of it. But these interests have shaped our fiscal policy too long.

Laurier and his reciprocity election campaigners

Stephen Leacock, economist, historian, and humorist. From The Great Victory in Canada, reprinted from The National Review, 1911.

The leader with his white plumes typified, as it were, purity and chivalry; his bilingual eloquence recalled the union of the two races on which the Canadian Commonwealth was built. Beside him was Sir Richard Cartwright, the Nestor of the Senate, whose views on Free Trade were known to be so profound that they figured, without further utterance, as a solid asset of a Protectionist government. Here, too, was Mr. Fielding the magician of the legend who could spin you a yearly surplus out of the palm of an empty hand as easily as a juggler twirls a billiard ball out of nothingness. Near him, lest the reproach of senility might be brought against a government growing grey in office, was Mr. Mackenzie King, a sometime economist now "gone bad" in politics, whose boyish countenance was useful as typifying the fire of youth and in its gentle moments was supposed to beam with all the rouguishness of political childhood. The debonair Mr. Fisher presided over agriculture and the weather, becoming, in the Liberal mythology, the hod of the Harvest, just as Mr. Pugsley had become the god of Wharves and Bridges and Sir Frederick Borden, from his repulse of the Fenians in 1866, the god of Scientific Warfare.

Laurier's call to the voters

Sir Wilfrid Laurier, excerpt from statement published in The Globe, Toronto, July 29, 1911.

The issue, my fellow countrymen, is in your hands, and to your decision His Majesty's Government in Canada are well content to leave it. It has been alleged by the Opposition that this Agreement, if consumated, would imperil Canada's connection with the Mother-country, and finally bring about the annexation of Canada to the United States. It is impossible to treat such an argument with any kind of respect, if, indeed, it can be dignified with the name of argument; for if it has any meaning, its meaning is that the people of Canada would be seduced from their allegiance by prosperity to follow the larger flow of natural products from this country to the other. Indeed, the very reverse would be the natural consequence, for the experience of all ages abundantly testifies that trade is ever the most potent agency of peace, amity, and mutual respect between nations.

Toronto Star advocates free trade with U.S.

Excerpts from Toronto Star editorial, September 18, 1911.

The men who are opposing reciprocity and men who do not understand Canada and the Canadians... The reciprocity party is in line with the stalwart Canadianism of the country. It has a spirit of hope, of courage, of unity, of progress... It is the party of sturdy, courageous patriotism. It is not afraid to trust Canadians. It does not believe that Canadians will abandon their flag and their country if they are allowed to trade more freely with the United States. That coward's advice, that craven fear, that distrust of Canadian patriotism comes from the opponents of reciprocity. Do not be too hard on them. They do not understand Canada and the Canadians.

In short, a bad thing

Ernest Charles Drury, co-founder of the United Farmers of Ontario and Premier of Ontario, 1919-1923. Excerpt from Forts of Folly: Are We Sane About Protection? Toronto, 1932: The Ryerson Press

...the Forts of Folly — the system of Canadian protectionism, born of political expediency, nurtured on corruption and prejudice, entrenched in politics and press; a system which has operated to retard national growth, and to oppress more than half our people; a system which has blossomed in arrogance, and borne fruits in unearned millions, in stock jobbery, in financial brigandage; a system whose beneficiaries, though they have received thousands of millions of dollars from the Canadian people in tariff favours, have shown themselves powerless to provide work for their employees, but have turned them out on the streets in scores of thousands.

The opportunity missed in 1948

John Deutsch, then a senior official in the Department of Finance, outlined the advantages of a contemplated free-trade agreement with the United States in a "top secret" memorandum in March, 1948, for Prime Minister Mackenzie King and some members of his cabinet and key officials. The following are excerpts from the memorandum, which is found in the Deutsch papers (file 5190), archives, Queen's University, Kingston, Ontario.

The present Canadian difficulties are due to the collapse of the United Kingdom-European leg of the traditional economic triangle upon which the Canadian economy has been built. In seeking to overcome these difficulties we must either (a) rely upon the possibility of restoring the financial ability of the United Kingdom and Western Europe to import from Canada upon a greatly enlarged scale, or (b) take positive steps by means of restrictions to substantially and permanently reduce the volume of imports from the United States and thereby endeavor to obtain our requirements from other sources at much higher costs; or (c) achieve a much higher degree of economic self-sufficiency; or (d) greatly expand our exports to the United States. The possibility of achieving the first alternative in an adequate way is doubtful, to say the least, and involves a very large measure of risk. The second and third alternatives would mean painful readjustments and a permanently lower standard of living. The fourth alternative, namely free access to the United States market, would mean a permanently greater economic integration with the United States. In assessing the implications of that greater integration, we must consider what would happen if the other alternatives fail. If they do, then economic dependence upon the United States is inevitable. The question, therefore, is should our future economic relations with the United States be established as soon as possible on a self-support basis through unrestricted access to markets, or should we run the risk of becoming an economic supplicant when our bargaining position is weak?...

We are asked... to consider what appears to be a unique opportunity at the present moment to establish our economic relationships with the United States on a self-supporting basis — the basis upon which nations must usually achieve the command of their own destiny. Should we seek to command our destiny on such a basis, or should we risk the great uncertainties involved in proceeding along the present course in the hope that the economic fabric which the war has torn apart will <u>ultimately</u> be re-established in its old forms.

.... it is the carefully considered conviction of those who have worked on the technical aspects of the present proposal that it is highly unlikely that such satisfactory terms, in both the economic and <u>political</u> sense, could again be obtained for Canada.

Economic strength = political strength

Harry Johnson, Professor of Economics, University of Chicago and The London School of Economics. Excerpts from testimony to the Standing Committee on Foreign Affairs, Ottawa, May 2, 1974.

The future of Canada lies in being as rich and powerful economically as possible. Our Achilles heel in the past has very often been that we opt for a lower standard of living and when that gets too tough we lose people. Anything that could raise the Canadian standard of living and give Canadians more resources to spend on being themselves would be an advantage. It is from that standpoint that I look at trade policy. I do not look at trade policy as a question of political involvement, but rather the opposite, that we can only be an independent nation if we can afford to pay our own way, and if we can afford to risk something on pursuing our own objectives. The worst situation for us is to be a very small, poor country right next to a rich one. We would be much better off, and better off than they are, if we were a rich country on a rich continent and able to carry our own responsibilities.

It is in that sense that I have been what I believe people call a continentalist. I do not like that kind of language. It seems to me that sending people to college for four years just so that they can learn to divide the world into continentalists and others is a waste of educational investment. I do not like the phrase; either it is a truisum — because we are on a continent, we cannot move off it; the best chance for us is as an efficient and profitable development of the continent as possible — or else it means that somehow I want to throw away Canadian individuality in favor of becoming an American, and I certainly do not want that...

... we are much more likely to want to become Americans — and this has been documented by past Canadian history — if our independence costs us so much. There comes a time when the average man would rather eat better than be independent. Independence usually means not that the average man is independent, but that you and the leaders of the country can be independent in your actions. However, when the average man finds that it is costing him too much in terms of the standard of living, he begins to vote with his feet. Our whole history of population development here has been to some extent serving as a half-way house to which Europeans frightened of America may come. Then they find that they are not so frightened after all and can cope, so they move on to where the big money is. I would like to see some of the big money in Canada.

It is complete nonsense to say that economic union leads to political union. The facts of history for hundreds of years show that there have been free trade arrangements without there being political union. And there have been lots of political unions without free trade arrangements.

My attitude is that we are most likely to go for political union when the world is so divided that we as a nation, which exports and trades in many different kinds of things, find ourselves cramped and our population suffering from discrimination. We will then throw in the towel and say, "If we either have to starve to death up here or join the United States and be rich, we will join the United States." ...we won't, if we can be reasonably well off without becoming American.

I see no forces in Canadian society that are strongly in favor of becoming American. I see no forces in the United States that want Canada to be part of the United States. I can see political union with the United States only as a result of some desperate effort by Canadians to save something for themselves in this disintegrating world.

That is why I think that in a sense free trade is the best guarantee we have against that, because free trade will guarantee us the opportunity to markets which we might otherwise not have, without meeting the cost of political union in order to gain access. When it is a choice between starving to death and giving up some independence, Canadians are not unique in preferring to live, and live reasonably well, rather than demonstrate for a political principle.

Economic Council measures the costs

Excerpts from a study by the Economic Council of Canada, Looking Outward, a New Trade Strategy for Canada. Ottawa, 1975.

Though not so extreme as in earlier years, our present commercial policy retains a strong element of protectionism, and Canadian exporters still face substantial trade barriers in foreign markets. Under the system of protection that has evolved, this country has remained by and large an exporter of natural resources and an importer of more highly manufactured products. This system has existed at a time when our trade has become increasingly concentrated on one major source and market — the United States.

The lingering protection in Canada and foreign countries still largely confines Canadian secondary industry to a relatively small market, and this has adverse effects on the growth and productivity and real income, as well as on the extent and pattern of foreign ownership, the pace of technological advance, and the development of innovative capability. In short, commercial policy has contributed to a deterioration of this country's capacity for sustained, dynamic, autonomous growth — a capacity that will become increasingly important in the future. Thus the results of a long evolution of trade policies can hardly be viewed as a contribution to independent national decision-making in Canada.

[Studies] confirm that the Canadian tariff of itself redistributes income from other parts of the country to Ontario and Quebec. This has contributed to a greater concentration of employment in the central provinces.

Canadian tariff protection has been a chronic source of contention in federal-provincial affairs. The Atlantic provinces and the west have never ceased to resent the price they must pay for the tariff and to suggest that its benefits accrue almost entirely to Ontario and Quebec.

...the onus cannot be placed wholly upon either past or present Canadian commercial policy. But its direct regional effects have often been negative. Furthermore, to the extent that it has caused inefficiencies in the economy, commercial policy has reduced the real resources available to deal with regional problems.

The Senators call for free trade

After several years of public hearings, the Senate Standing Committee on Foreign Affairs, under the chairmanship of Senator George C. van Roggen, urged a free trade agreement with the United States in a report issued in August, 1978. Following are excerpts from the report, Canada-United States Relations, volume 11, Canada's Trade Relations with the United States.

Starting from the perception that serious measures have to be taken to improve Canada's competitive capacity, the committee has considered each of Canada's principal options:

• It rejects increased protection as leading inevitably to diminished competitiveness and a declining standard of living.

• It supports general tariff reductions under the GATT, on condition that nontariff measures are equally and effectively dismantled, but is skeptical regarding the effectiveness of the results expected to emerge from the multilateral trade talks.

• It sees no prospect for general free trade and counsels against any suggestion of moving toward unilateral free trade. The preferred arrangement for Canada would be to negotiate sectoral free trade arrangements with the U.S. where there would be a benefit to Canada in doing so, but it is unlikely that such an approach would be of interest to the U.S. unless it were as a first step toward bilateral free trade.

In order to resist the gradual shift of Canadian manufacturing capacity to the U.S. and to strengthen potentially competitive firms and industries in Canada, Canadians should seriously examine the benefits to be derived from free trade with the U.S. It is not a policy without risk, but the committee is convinced that the balance of advantage is greater than most witnesses perceived...

On the economic side, the weak competitive position of the Canadian economy would result, even with extensive adjustment schemes, in serious dislocation of Canadian secondary manufacturing. But bilateral free trade with the U.S. appears to offer in the long run the most effective approach to overcome the economic problems which Canada is facing.

Bilateral free trade in North America has often been presented as heading inevitably to the economic and cultural assimilation of Canada by the U.S.

The committee disagrees. Having presented reports in 1973 on the necessity of developing more intensive Canadian relations with the European Community and in 1972 on the need to expand relations with Japan, the committee is fully aware of the importance of these extra-continental relationships. But an effort to expand these connections is not inconsistent with pursuit of the long-term goal of free trade with the U.S. An economically strong Canada is in a much better situation to maintain political and cultural independence than an economically weak Canada.

In the short term, the Quebec political situation precludes an immediate initiative. But the prospect of a free trade arrangement between Canada and the U.S. raises an interesting perspective. On the one hand, Quebec would have little economically to offer Canada which had access to the entire U.S. market; on the other hand, the cost to Quebec of being outside such an arrangement would be enormous, and not only in economic terms. From the point of view of both Canada and the U.S., a policy which would lead to a strengthening of Canadian unity would be an important non-economic benefit to be derived from pursuit of the bilateral free trade objective.

The committee urges governments in Canada, as well as the business and labor communities, to assess without prejudice Canada's present economic prospects, the alternative solutions and their consequences. The committee recommends that they consider seriously the option of bilateral free trade with the U.S.

Macdonald Commission's leap of faith

Royal Commission on the Economic Union and Development Prospects for Canada. Ottawa, August, 1985. Excerpt from the summary, and from the Conclusions and Recommendations.

At the very heart of our Report is a call to all Canadians to look outward to the opportunities and challenges in the world, to place greater reliance on market forces than on governments in matters of economic development, to renew the spirit of compassion and effectiveness that has marked the development of our social policies, and to render the three institutions of our state — responsible parliamentary government, federalism and the Charter of Rights and Freedoms — more responsible and democratic.

... better and more secure access to the U.S. market represents a basic requirement, while denials of that access is an ever-present threat. We are extremely vulnerable to any strengthening of U.S. protectionism. Early bilateral negotiations with the United States could provide opportunities for the two countries to negotiate reduction or elimination of tariff and other barriers to cross-border trade, at a pace and on a scale not likely to be achieved multilaterally in a further GATT round. Such negotiations could also be used to win agreement on rules designed to deal with special or unique problems affecting cross-border trade; they would provide a more secure shield against a U.S. policy of protection.

We believe that Canada/U.S. free trade is not at odds with efforts to strengthen and improve the existing multilateral framework. Rather, Commissioners see it as a complementary approach, involving concentration of efforts and scarce resources on our most important market. We see multilateral negotiations proceeding in parallel. In our view, such a two-tiered approach is the best way to ensure that Canadian industry will win sufficient access to foreign markets to invest and grow with confidence. At the same time, it will allow us to open our market in an orderly fashion and thus ensure that trade policy does its part in encouraging the development of a more competitive and productive economy.

Commissioners see negotiations with the United States as neither panacea nor disaster, but as a prudent course which will help make us richer and, making us richer, strengthen the fabric of our country and increase our self-confidence. While this course may initially make Canada more dependent on the U.S. market, it will offer our nation a more secure relationship and thus make us less vulnerable. Ultimately, it should strengthen and diversify our economy, achieving for us goals that we have long sought, but which have eluded us, largely because our domestic manufacturing sector has been too weak to attain them.

PART TWO:
THE DOLLARS AND SENSE

Chapter three:
Manufacturers itch to
compete for U.S. sales

J. Laurent Thibault
Charles Hantho
Barbara Caldwell

Mr. Thibault is president of The Canadian Manufacturers' Association; Mr. Hantho is chairman of the association and chairman of C-I-L Inc; Ms Caldwell is a member of the association, and president of Cleanwear Products. Excerpts from their presentation to the House of Commons committee on external affairs and international trade, Ottawa, November 18, 1987.

Thibault: we've come a long way

No other issue has been discussed more thoroughly within the CMA than the issue of free trade for quite some time now... the archives of the CMA show that in 1871 when the CMA was created, our customs committee wrote the first schedule of tariffs, which Sir John A. Macdonald, we are told, promptly proceeded to adopt as one of the elements of the National Policy.

You have seen our brief and you know that the CMA, and indeed the manufacturing community, has come a long way since those days... I think it is important for the committee to know that we find the manufacturing community very supportive of this agreement, right across the country. We find it quite ironic that despite statements by a number of people in politics who are against the agreement, they certainly do not reflect the views of the manufacturing community in our forums across the country.

The manufacturing community is the sector that will have to deal with what really is the heart of this issue. Obviously, the support in a broadly-based organization like the CMA, with thousands of members across the country, could never be 100 percent unanimous, but the consensus nevertheless, I think, is very strong and very positive.

I think there is a sense of confidence in the manufacturing community that this agreement and the further opening up of the market with the United States create some very important opportunities for us as well as some very important challenges. People seem to have a great deal of confidence that the transition is manageable and a great deal of confidence that, as we have been for many years, we can and will compete in a more liberalized environment.

Hantho: We cannot afford a Fort Canada mentality

We believe the Canada-U.S. trade agreement is a sound foundation for the future. I guess the subset to that is that Canadian manufacturing can compete and is competing in the global environment...

The problem with this debate, in some sense, is that it is seen as a very massive step change. Actually, it is part of an evolution.

In order to ensure its future growth, the central objective of Canadian manufacturing in the negotiations was to obtain a substantial improvement in our effective access to the U.S. market and greater security of this access. Manufacturers need to see the possibility of growth into the larger market in order to justify the key investments in sophisticated advanced technology that they need to stay in the forefront of their industry. We cannot afford a Fort Canada mentality.

In this regard, a core element of access was the removal of tariffs. This was accomplished in the deal. Many Canadian companies have indicated that removal of these tariffs will allow them to fully rationalize their operations and substantially improve productivity during the 10-year phase-in period. From the point of view of our ultimate objective, to improve competitiveness, the removal of tariffs need not be seen as a negative development, as is commonly portrayed in the popular press.

Manufacturing has been adjusting well to the continuous lowering of these trade barriers over the last four decades, and every single industrial manufacturer has sharply increased his ability to export, while at the same time he has had to rationalize by importing products in which he is not competitive.

In terms of jobs gained and lost in the process of adjustment, there has always been a continuous relatively large in-flow and out-flow of employment in the manufacturing sector. To keep this potential impact of the 10-year period of adjustment in perspective, it is important to note that there are many powerful and sudden forces affecting manufacturing. These include massive shifts in exchange rates, in some markets as much as 50 percent in 12 to 24 months. Just look at the recent currency changes. The magnitude of those changes can swamp the kind of residual tariffs that we are eliminating.

Also, there is rapid technology change, large changes in consumer preferences, and normal economic cycles. In other words, manufacturers are continuing to adjust to an awful lot of things. For example, in the 1981 downturn, manufacturing employment in Canada dropped by some 300,000 jobs within a period of 15 months and did not recover those for several years. In the context of this, then, the potential job displacement that may result will be compensated for by new jobs created in other fields. Overall, the gradual tariff reduction seems manageable. In fact, economic theory and all the evidence indicates that the process of tariff reduction is precisely what releases consumer income, which in turn generates new demand, increased economic output, investment and employment. Canadian firms and workers have shown themselves to be more adaptive than is generally understood, and the potential benefits from increased exports provides both an incentive and the means to continue the restructuring of the Canadian economy.

In terms of our major goal of securing more assured access to the U.S. market, we did not seek, nor was it realistic to expect, exemption from each other's trade remedy laws. The key to mutually assured access is a dispute settlement mechanism that ensures better management of our trading relationship. It provides for the creation of bi-national panels that would make binding judgments on disputes about the terms of the agreement and on the application of each other's trade laws. The panel procedure applies particularly to anti-dumping and countervailing duty cases. This establishes the central principle that protects us from unilateral interpretation of U.S. laws and from blatant political manipulation.

What we did not get was a new set of rules, but we did get a commitment to write such a set within five to seven years. We did not, then, fully obtain our objective, and have only limited appeal on the substantive questions. However, we gain the important principle that the U.S. now allows another country to have a voice in the application of its trade remedy laws and the prospect of jointly formulated and enforced rules. This a valuable step forward that moves the dispute settlement to a binational body of trade experts instead of courts and lawyers. It should also limit the capricious and politically motivated abuses of their system.

In addition to having a voice in the application of trade remedy laws, implementation of the agreement may mean that U.S. trade legislation must contain a specific recognition of trade relations between the two countries. This means an end to the problem of Canada being unintentionally included in action directed by the U.S. against other countries.

While we did not get all we wanted in the first agreement, it represents substantial progress in the right direction, with a strong commitment to continue working at the remaining issues. It offers an anchor of rationality we can hang on to in turbulent protectionist waters. It also offers continued increases in our standard of living and the removal of many of the historical, regional tensions between western and central Canada. Canadian consumers will be clear beneficiaries, through lower prices and increased choice of goods.

Caldwell: nervous plunge only choice for small business

There are, of course, many types of small manufacturers with a host of different characteristics in Canada. But I think there are areas were we have common interests, and it is those that I should like to speak to.

Over the past year or so I have had the opportunity to speak to many of my colleagues on the subject of the free trade agreement. The reactions are varied, and they include nervousness and concern about the resources that we as business owners will require to access new market niches. And many of us have difficulty understanding the details of the agreement.

On the plus side is excitement and the anticipation of new opportunities. Regardless of the outcome of the negotiations, we are none of us in the same place we were before the trade talks began. Each of us has been given the boot in the pants, so to speak, that we needed to look at ourselves in a global context, to set aside our parochial view of the marketplace and to look at not just the U.S. but other markets as well, and to work toward global competitiveness.

The improved access in the agreement stemming from the elimination of tariffs and the removal of other trade restrictions will make small to medium-sized manufacturers more aware of the potential benefits of exporting to the United States. I do not mean to downplay the costs of adjustments. The fact is that as an owner of a small firm, one that manufactures clothing, I personally know my workforce and I know their concerns. I understand how traumatic it can be to lose a job. However, this is sometimes unavoidable.

Changes in the trading environment pose less of a threat to employment than technological change, to shifts in consumer preferences, to the emergence of new competitors, or exchange or interest rate fluctuations. Change is inevitable in business, and is often uncomfortable. Employees generally adopt the attitude of their employer or the person they look to as their leader. If the people upon whom these new policies will impact the most can be assured that programs are in place to help them adjust through retraining, or through social programs for those who are not capable of making the transition, the comfort level rises. We can then get on with the job of increasing our productivity to make us competitive in this new marketplace.

The public debate over this agreement usually ends up in an argument about whether Canada can maintain a separate and distinct identity. This has always been a concern and will be one, I think, as long as we live next door to the U.S. However, the U.S. is not going to go away and neither is Canada. Our sense of ourselves is deeply rooted in history and geography, and through hard work we have created a proud and prosperous country.

Closer commercial relations are not going to change our view of ourselves, or for that matter our view of the U.S. Speaking at a very personal level, while I have concern about the particular vulnerability of my own business, I do not frankly believe that the status quo is an option. Small manufacturers, indeed all manufacturers, must look much farther afield for opportunities to grow, and I welcome the opportunity free trade will provide.

Chapter four:
a stronger Canada with more
freedom and more choices

Simon Reisman

Mr. Reisman is a special Ambassador for Canada, and Chief Trade Negotiator. From an address to a combined meeting of the Canadian Club of Toronto and the Empire Club of Canada, Toronto, October 16, 1987.

Let me assure you, in the strongest possible terms, that what we achieved is good news. It is a good deal for Canada. And nothing, not even the lawyers who will translate it into their own special language, will change that.

Reaching an agreement was a historic occasion; historic in terms of Canada-U.S. relations, historic in the development of international trade relations, and historic in its unprecedented achievement of stability and the rule of law in trade relations between sovereign states.

What we achieved will, I am certain, stand as the largest trade deal ever negotiated between two countries. Now that is only fitting. Canada and the United States, after all, are the world's largest trading partners.

What we have achieved is a good deal for both countries — and that is important. For the deal to last, both countries must be satisfied that they have met their national interests; both countries must benefit; both must be able to say that they have made things better. And I believe we did that. This is a win-win agreement.

Only a juvenile delinquent, as the Prime Minister reminded me, believes that you can make an agreement in which you get all the benefits and your partner gets none. Fortunately, in matters of trade, given the benefits to be received from upgrading and obtaining better productivities, both sides can benefit — and I think we've done that.

The agreement will make us richer and more able to pursue the finer things of life. It will lead to a richer Canada, a Canada more able to maintain a strong safety net of social programs, vigorous regional and economic development programs, and a vibrant Canadian culture.

Those things the scare mongers insisted were at risk in these negotiations were not only never at risk, but they were fully protected. We fully safeguarded those areas most sensitive to Canadians and unique to the Canadian way of life.

More than three years ago, long before I took on the challenge of negotiating this agreement, I told a conference at the Brookings Institute in Washington the following:

> If the United States and Canada were able to work out a free trade agreement it would be a good thing for both countries and a good example for the world. It would make both countries richer. It would also make us better neighbors because it would remove many of the irritants about which we have been squabbling for many years. A free trade arrangement would not weaken Canadian sovereignty or the Canadian resolve to remain independent. Indeed, by enriching Canada, and by raising its confidence and its performance, an agreement would strengthen Canada's purpose and its ability to survive as a strong, free nation.

I believed that then, and I believe it even more today. At that time I did not believe it possible for this dream to come true during my life time, and I said so. I certainly didn't believe that I would be asked to negotiate one.

But it did. And I can tell you that I am a partisan, and a passionate believer in free trade. I'm not a political partisan, but I'm most partisan about this issue. I reject the pessimism and fears of the proponents of a little Canada who wish to hide behind protectionist walls under the guise of nationalism. I am a proud Canadian and confident in my belief that Canadians can compete with the very best.

But not with one hand tied behind their backs. What this agreement will do is cut the shackles of protectionism and fear. It will allow Canadian entrepreneurs, many of whom are in this room, to roll up their sleeves and take on the world as never before. And I know they will succeed.

We entered the negotiations to achieve two broad objectives. We sought a bigger market and a more secure market. The government sought to give Canadian manufacturers secure access to markets of some 250 million people so they could plan to invest with confidence. We achieved both those goals: a more open market, and a more secure market.

I believe that this agreement, if it's approved by Congress and by the Parliament of Canada, will create a whole new environment in which Canadians will work and live. It will affect their opportunity for jobs. It will affect the kind of work they do. It will affect the incomes they earn. It will affect the size of our population in a positive way. It will, I am confident, create a positive, constructive kind of environment with new opportunities for expansion and growth.

By the time this agreement takes full effect a decade from now, the average Canadian is going to find that he has more money in his pocket, and a wider choice of competitively priced goods and services on which to spend that money. And he will find, too, that he has a better job, a more interesting job, a more secure job — and he will be getting paid more to do it. Now if we can do that — and I believe this agreement will help us do that — I think you will agree that that is no mean achievement.

The agreement is particularly significant for the younger people, for our children and grandchildren. I don't know that it will affect me

> *Some Americans will have to swallow hard before accepting the method set up to settle trade disputes.*

very much at my age, other than to know that I had a part to play in getting it. But it will certainly affect my children and my grandchildren; what they will work at, what incomes they will earn, how they will spend it, and their willingness to stay in Canada and make their careers here. I believe all this will have a positive effect upon them.

Over the next few months, debate will rage in Canada, based on two visions of our country. One is of an open Canada, a confident Canada where our people can stand up and compete with the best. The other is of a country that tries to shelter behind a wall of protection that looks to the past rather than the future. It really comes down to whether you have confidence in the country and its people, its prospects, and its abilities; or whether you are frightened, insecure and afraid to get out there and compete.

Having said this agreement is good for Canada and meets the main objectives set by the government, what does it do, and how will it do it?

Quite apart from the size of markets and volume of trade affected, this agreement is precedent setting in the range of issues covered. We've agreed to eliminate all tariffs between us. This will be phased in, as many of you know, in stages, and all this was decided in close consultation with Canadian industry. I know it is conventional wisdom to say that the tariff matters little today, but don't you believe it. By removing the tariff on both sides of the border on thousands of items traded between Canada and the United States, we will give Canadian industry new opportunities. It will increase the competitiveness of Canadian exports ranging from petrochemicals to furniture. It will lower costs to Canadian consumers of everything from food and wine to machinery and computers.

We will establish improved conditions for trade in agriculture — all tariffs are eliminated. There will be new opportunities for exporters of beef, veal and pork — a major priority in western Canada.

On trade in energy — and I think the energy chapter is perhaps the best chapter in the agreement — we've agreed to reciprocal concessions to remove barriers to trade in oil, gas, electricity and uranium. Our objective was to assure the freest possible bilateral trade in energy. With this agreement we will have secured our access to the U.S. market for Canadian energy exports, something we have sought to do for many, many decades....

At the same time we've maintained our ability, should we judge there to be a real need, to take measures to prevent the over-exploitation of Canada's non-renewable energy resources, and to make sure that Canadians have an adequate supply.

It stands to reason that if we want free and secure access for our energy products that we agree not to abuse our best customer should a real shortage situation develop. We already have similar commitments under the International Energy Agency. That is what good trading partners do for one another. They do not short them unfairly in times of need.

We've also agreed to remove and reduce barriers to trade and investment in services. We've established, for the first time ever, a contractual code of rules to cover trade in services. Any new measures taken by either government will in future have to conform to the reciprocal undertaking to extend national treatment to each other. Additionally, we've made some progress in rolling back existing barriers in financial services, enhanced telecommunications, architectural services, tourism, and one or two other sectors. More such technical accords will probably be reached in the future as the agreement looks forward to further progress along those lines.

We've agreed to provide for a more certain and open investment regime, while preserving our right to review significant takeovers and maintain important Canadian ownership requirements that are now in place, through grandfathering. We have a specific agreement which facilitates travel for business and service personnel between the two countries. Canadians will be able to sell and service their sales as never before — and that is a very important achievement, as all of you know who have been harassed at the border when you went over to do business.

We did not get the big procurement deal that we sought, because the Americans weren't ready. They were not ready to take on little Canada!

But we made a start. Federal procurement rules will be eased. This will open about $650 million in Canadian contracts to U.S. bids, and almost $4 billion in U.S. contracts to Canadian bids. The two countries have also committed themselves to further easing of procurement rules in the future.

All these commitments will lead to a more open exchange of goods and services between us, and a more rational pattern of investment. By eliminating barriers at both borders, we will both emerge winners. In both countries, industry will be able to specialize and increase productivity.

But Canada also wanted secure access. Canadians wanted to be sure that when they invested to serve the North American market they would not be subject to the whims of American courts and American regulators. They wanted a fair deal. They complained that U.S. trade laws were being used capriciously to harass them. They had lost confidence in the fairness of these laws. And without such security, investors will inevitably be attracted to the safety of the larger market.

The United States is now on a protectionist tide. That is not going to be reversed soon. The new omnibus trade bill, when it comes out, will be in a protectionist direction. The choice for Canadians is to be on the inside of that wall, or on the outside. Most Americans believe that Canadians are fair traders. We're not the main target of their complaints about being treated unfairly. But their anger and their anxiety have sideswiped us and given too many opportunities to those who have a bone to pick with us and find us a little too competitive.

In general, trade law and practice, both national and international, affords far greater rights and protection to domestic producers than to exporters and consumers. What we've now achieved is a significant step toward correcting this imbalance.

And we've done it in this way. The two governments have agreed to a unique dispute settlement procedure that guarantees fair interpretation and impartial application of their respective anti-dumping and countervailing duty laws. It provides an insurance policy that introduces accountability to U.S. regulators and investigators. In effect, we have established a watch dog to ensure that the laws are interpreted fairly and applied properly and that there be no arbitrariness in the application of those laws.

New limits are also placed on the use of emergency trade laws against import charges, with binding arbitration there as well, if necessary. Now either government may seek a review of an anti-dumping or countervailing duty determination by a bilateral panel with binding powers. Disputes with the U.S. will be assessed on the basis of U.S. law; those with Canada, on the basis of Canadian law. Since this joint review will replace existing rights to appeal to our respective federal courts, this procedure will not add yet another level of litigation to the already complex system of trade remedy laws. Moreover, such a panel will be oriented toward practical, commercial policy considerations rather than fine points of law, and that's by virtue of the composition that these tribunals will have.

The success of this review procedure will not be counted in the number of times it is evoked, but in the number of petitions it discourages and the number of politically-inspired decisions that it halts. That, after all, is the essence of a successful watchdog.

This system constitutes a very strong beginning, but we've also agreed that in the next several years, Canada and the United States will develop "a substitute system of laws in both countries for antidumping and countervailing duties." It is intended that by 1996 at the latest, U.S. and Canadian trade laws respecting each other will be replaced by mutually-developed North American trade rules, which we will develop together. Within 10 years of entering trade negotiations the existing system of unilateral laws, unilaterally interpreted and enforced, will be replaced by jointly formulated rules, jointly enforced, within North America.

A Canada-U.S. Trade Commission will manage the agreement. No new laws affecting bilateral trade between the two countries may be passed without consultation and joint review and amendment if necessary. And this will take effect after January 1, 1989 when the agreement comes into effect. For the period between now and when the agreement enters into force, we have agreed to a standstill. We've agreed that to the fullest extent possible, both countries would behave as if the agreement were already in force.

While Americans, I hope, will see this agreement as mutually beneficial, there are many Americans, including Congressmen and Senators, who many of us have spoken to, who will want to complete this deal with Canada, and we believe they will succeed in overcoming the opposition. But some will have to swallow hard on the question of the apparatus we put in place to settle disputes. For the first time in history, for the first time ever, the Americans have accepted the idea that a binational institution with a neutral chairman, or a neutral judge, will be the ultimate appeal against sanctions by them under their law. Now that's very big. They will see this as a major, major step. But I'm confident that when they see it in its proper perspective, they will accept it as eminently fair and reasonable as a basis for settling differences between two neighbors and two friends.

Canadians will come to realize that it is a major step for this great

44

power, the United States of America, 10 times the size of Canada in population, a major world power, to agree with its neighbor that in the end, in the last analysis, if a dispute develops between us that dispute will be resolved by the two countries jointly and with a neutral chairman to be the judge.

And what of the nay-sayers, the scare mongers? Do they have a point? They said we would bargain away our culture; that we would put our social programs in this, that we would give away our right to promote regional development, that we would destroy Canada's farm

---

Save $800 per family per year

Harvie Andre, federal minister of consumer and corporate affairs, from a letter in the Financial Post, February 29, 1988.

My department's findings, which are consistent with independent research, indicate that the average Canadian household will save approximately $800 per year once the agreement is fully implemented. This direct consumer benefit from the agreement results from the elimination of customs tariffs on imports of U.S. consumer goods... [While] 75 percent of imports from the U.S. are currently duty free... tariffs on consumer goods are on average three times higher than tariffs on other imports from the U.S. Because of tariffs as high as 25 percent, some U.S. consumer goods are simply not presently available in Canada.

---

marketing system and — unkindest cut of all — that I would gut the Auto Pact.

They turned out to be wrong, misinformed, and mischievous. The agreement safeguards areas sensitive to Canadians. And have they recanted? No. They continue to whine, and shilly-shally and misinform and misinterpret.

The agreement does not threaten Canada's social programs. Indeed, as I said repeatedly, social programs were never at issue. What we have achieved, however, will make Canadians more able to afford quality social programs for all Canadians. You know, you have to more than want good programs — you've got to be able to pay for them. And that comes out of hard work and productivity and entrepreneurship and trade.

The agreement will not in any way limit the capacity of the government to nurture Canada's cultural industries and policies. We have safeguarded fully our right in Canada to pursue our unique, cultural patterns, behavior and objectives. Again, there was never any question that the agreement would undermine Canada's cultural identity. And again, the wealth that this agreement will generate will benefit Canadian support for the arts and our cultural industries.

On the issue of regional development, and the question of subsidies, we shall continue to be able to pursue and promote our programs of regional development in Atlantic Canada and the west, regions of the country that have unique problems and potential possibilities. We have safeguarded our right in Canada to combat regional disparities. This is such a fundamental part of the essence of Canada that one has to question the motives of people who cried wolf about this one. What in the world did they hope to achieve?

The agreement does not threaten the automotive industry. In fact, the essential features of the Auto Pact — duty free access to the United States — will be more secure in a comprehensive deal that also stiffens North American content requirements. The Auto Pact is preserved, and we've agreed on rules of origin which will provide new opportunities for employment and production in North America in this vital sector. Both domestic and offshore assemblers and producers of parts can prosper under the new arrangement. We honored our pledge that we would retain the Auto Pact and only entertain suggestions which would make things better.

The agreement exempts Canadian brewers. This is a mixed blessing. I am aware of the higher cost structure faced by the Canadian brewing industry, but I would hope that once interprovincial barriers to trade in beer have been removed, Canadians will want to see the benefits of open trade and competition extended to this industry. This isn't a threat — it's a hope.

The agreement does not threaten agricultural marketing boards or the supply management system, but it does give Canada's farmers better and more secure access to the richest market in the world. I am referring particularly to livestock and red meats, so vital to our western economy.

Now the Prime Minister made it clear from the outset, when he asked me to take on this job, that we did not want a deal for the sake of a deal. We wanted an agreement that reflects a clear Canadian bottom line, in terms of what we needed and what we were not prepared to negotiate. He set that out in the clearest possible terms, and I must say I never had more complete contact with a Prime Minister in all the years I served in Ottawa. I guess we spoke at least 40 times on the phone, and we met at least 15 or more times because he kept very close touch with us. I think we met his bottom line and we met the bottom line for all Canadians.

That led to some agonizing decisions. But in the end the government made the right choices, we got a good deal, a balanced deal and a fair deal. The process is not over, but we have dealt with the major elements and the results are overwhelmingly positive.

May I interject a personal note here. I considered the Prime Minister's confidence in me a great honor. For someone who worked for 40 years to open markets and reduce barriers it is a singular distinction to be allowed to, at the end of my career, have an opportunity to negotiate this agreement. And I very much appreciated having this opportunity. I want to say that it was a good team effort. Throughout the piece I had the support of a first-class group of dedicated Canadians who shared my dream....

But the real honor should go to the Prime Minister. The real honor goes to Brian Mulroney, who had the vision and the courage to take this initiative and to see this challenge through to the successful negotiation of the agreement. This is his agreement, and he has earned his place in history, come what may.

But it's not just an agreement for Canada and the United States, it is an agreement which strikes out against protectionism worldwide. It is an example to the world and a catalyst for the Uruguay round of multilateral trade negotiations. What we have achieved together bilaterally we will seek to carry forward with all of our trading partners at the GATT table in Geneva. Protectionist and inward looking forces in both countries will now try to mobilize to defeat this historic agreement. They will not succeed. It is a political fact that the forces of protectionism are generally more focused, more vocal, and better organized than interests that benefit from freer trade. But their fears will not withstand the dedication and vision of those who see a great future for Canada.

On two occasions over the last century, similar initiatives have been defeated by the forces of protectionism, nationalism and negativism. This time, the hard work and determination of those who prefer competition and challenge to protection and restrictions will ensure that this historic initiative comes to fruition. The rest of the world is not standing still. We cannot afford to rest on our laurels if we wish to survive and prosper in the next century. Our country faces a historic challenge. Let us take it. Let us face it, and move forward together.

Chapter five:
firmer cornerstones for
our standard of living

John D. Herrick

Mr. Herrick is chairman of the Canadian Chamber of Commerce. From an address to the Canadian Club of Toronto, October 19, 1987.

Business in Canada must realize that it cannot hope to retain its own markets at home if it does not aggressively pursue opportunities abroad; and it also must realize that it cannot hope to supply all parts of all markets.

In a trading environment of world product mandates and increasing global competitiveness, Canada must be ready and able to adjust to the challenges and opportunities of a world market. Business must be positioned to identify appropriate and sustainable market niches, adopt to the newest technologies and develop economies of scale.

International competitiveness is the catchword of the 1980s and will continue into the 1990s. A more competitive Canadian business community will mean increased domestic employment and a higher standard of living for Canadians from all parts of Canada.

The question is, how do we translate the concept into concrete, tangible results. Well, it requires a number of inter-related parts.

It needs a framework of domestic fiscal and economic policies conducive to liberalizing trade; it requires co-operation and accommodation with our trading partners; it needs a world trading order open for business; and finally, it needs the wherewithal of an informed business community willing to take risks. And let there be no mistake about it — Canada's future prosperity depends on its ability to trade in goods, services and investments in the markets of the world.

In a recent forecast of the world economy, the United Nations predicted stagnating incomes in Latin America, declining ones in Africa, little hope for third world debtor countries, and continued high unemployment in western Europe. Rising protectionism in the United States poses an equally serious threat to the world trading order.

These trends, combined with slow growth in the overall global economy, in the order of 2.5 to 3.5 percent, point to the daunting challenge which lies ahead for both developing and developed countries to reach important compromises and accommodations of their national priorities.

The new round of multilateral trade negotiations under the GATT will attempt to forge a better understanding among the 94 signatory countries in such areas as tariff and non-tariff barriers to trade, dispute settlement, the functioning of the GATT itself and, for the first time, investment, services and agriculture. The Canadian government has been working hard to secure early progress in this most important round.

Canadian business has its own network of multilateral organizations through which it can promote Canadian interests and relay Canadian concerns. The Canadian Chamber of Commerce is a founding member of the International Business Council of Canada. The IBCC is the Canadian business group that officially consults with the key inter-governmental bodies influencing international business. It presents Canadian business views to the OECD as the Canadian member of the Business and Industry Advisory Committee.

As the Canadian member of the International Chamber of Commerce, it confers with various U.N. bodies, such as the World Bank, the International Monetary Fund, and the GATT. And it participates as the Canadian member of the international organization of employers to the International Labor Organization. These are all important and largely under-utilized links that the Canadian business community has with other trading nations.

So the Chamber clearly recognizes the importance of co-operation at both business and government levels in multilateral fora in pursuing Canadian business objectives. It also understands the value of bilateral and regional associations.

The Chamber promotes business interests through a number of bilateral councils, including: the Canada-Korea Business Council; the Canada-India Business Council; the Committee on Canada-United States relations; and the recently opened trade office in Taiwan. The Chamber also promotes Canadian business activities in regional associations through its management of the Canada-Arab business council, Canadian-East European Trade Council, its involvement with the Asian Canada Business Council, and its very recent initiative to manage the Canadian Council for the Americas.

I have spoken briefly about the Chamber's role in international organizations because it is perhaps not as well known. The traditional connection people make with the Chamber is that of a large and active business association which monitors federal issues, solicits the views of the Canadian business community, and communicates them to policy makers in Ottawa. Current membership in the Canadian Chamber exceeds 170,000.

Given its full support for international business co-operation through multilateral, regional and bilateral groups, the Canadian Chamber of Commerce looks very favorably upon the successfully concluded bilateral deal with the United States. In fact, the Chamber has been a long-standing and ardent proponent of such a deal long before it became fashionable because of protectionist sentiment in the U.S. and political impetus in Canada.

While we are in full support of the agreement, we do not see the deal as a panacea for Canada, nor as an end in itself. Rather, we see it as a positive step in the country's long-term goal of enhanced domestic productivity and improved international competitiveness — the cornerstones to our standard of living.

Even some of the so-called "sensitive sectors," such as textiles, speak positively of the agreement — not because the exercise is without risks, but because the opportunities presented by their improved access to a larger market will help them to better compete with the pressure in their domestic market from offshore sources.

I'd like also to say a word about some of the opponents of the agreement. One thing was certain before the ink was dry on the deal, and that was that the opposition was going to be critical of any *deal,* regardless of the outcome. Their public refrains have been predictable and quite unspectacular. Opposition to a great extent has focused on the supposed assault of our sovereignty.

They would have us not embrace our southern neighbor commercially for fear of being gobbled up politically and culturally. This appears to us to be a little nonsensical. In fact, this issue is already largely behind us. Whether we like it or not, Canada is already deep in the economic embrace of the United States. We have not sacrificed any of our culture, self-identity or political sovereignty in the process. Why should opponents to the deal question our resolve or ability as a people to remain Canadian? Canadians don't. We know who we are and what we cherish and none of that has been threatened in the least by the agreement.

It is fair to say that any association between two or more parties will reduce to a degree each party's ability to act independently. But, as I have stated, such accommodations are taking place and are desirable today at all levels in order to secure stable and beneficial trading relationships.

Finally on this subject, while the views of many of the deal's opponents have been largely predictable, it is much more difficult to understand the behavior of the Ontario government. It is prudent to review the fine print once the experts have drafted the text and reserve formal commitments until that time.

But let's not lose sight of the potential an agreement holds out for Canada and Canadians from all regions. The U.S. currently provides 83 percent of Ontario's imports and takes 90 percent of all her exports. The benefits of a more stable arrangement for Ontario should be self-evident. Of all provinces, Ontario, benefiting as it does from the auto pact, an outstanding example of a trade deal with the Americans, should appreciate the benefits more secure access to the U.S. market can bring.

There are many positive benefits to Ontario. I can only hope that

> **The benefits will depend on our ability to take advantage of enormous opportunities in the U.S. -- and in the markets of the world.**

once the agreement is reviewed in detail the province will take a more positive and progressive view of the package.

Before concluding, I want to talk about the negotiations respecting a dispute settlement mechanism. We were not able to obtain what we had initially hoped for in this area, and frankly, I think our expectations were a little high, given the current climate of the U.S. Congress. What we sought was greater discipline by Americans on the use of U.S. countervail and anti-dumping laws.

Much was made in the press, partly as a result of the Prime Minister's public declarations, of the need for a **binding** binational tribunal to adjudicate trade disputes falling under these sections of U.S. trade law. If you are going to ask a tribunal to pass judgments, however, you have to give it a body of law or a set of rules from which to work.

And, as many negotiators around the world have found, particularly in the GATT, it's not easy to write a set of rules governing the use of subsidies between sovereign states. The GATT has been at it for 16 years. Mr. Reisman and Mr. Murphy had 16 months to reach an understanding of what constitutes a subsidy, and to agree to a set of mutually applied rules governing their use in both countries: a challenge which proved impossible in time to meet the October deadline.

Joint rules were not possible, so the mechanism that has been agreed to under the terms of the free trade agreement will have to use the existing rules of each country. Again, this is not what we had hoped for, but it is better than what we have now.

Furthermore, the agreement does not turn a blind eye to the progress that was made on subsidies and it does recognize the value of establishing clear rules for their use. For the next five years and possibly seven, both sides will continue to work toward a workable set of rules which will add greater teeth to the binding binational body set in place by the current agreement.

In addition, the agreement also stipulates that once the deal comes into force on January 1, 1989, changes in anti-dumping and countervail duty legislation can only apply to each country following consultations and only if specifically provided for in the new legislation. Even then, either country can ask the tribunal to review such changes in light of the object and purpose of the agreement and their rights and obligations under the GATT anti-dumping and subsidies code.

The agreement also allows for non-trade related items to be brought to a binational process to have disputes settled, such as disputes regarding the interpretation and application of the agreement.

Finally, there is an important standstill provision, which draws on the full weight and spirit of the agreement, to dissuade any action which might jeopardize the agreement's approval process, ie, the omnibus U.S. trade bill.

These changes, while not reaching the ultimate goals of some Canadians, represent an important step forward, both symbolically and substantively, in establishing a more secure trading relationship with our American neighbors. Failure to secure an agreement would have left us exposed to direct and indirect attacks on our exports from an increasingly militant Congress, and we would have lost the many opportunities available to Canada in other areas of the agreement.

In conclusion, the deal is not without risks, but nothing is worth having if you are not willing to take risks — calculated, pragmatic risks. Adjustments will be required on both sides of the border but the phase-in provisions and existing government support programs should help to minimize disruption and dislocation of those affected.

The benefits to be gained will not be felt overnight and will largely depend on the ability and willingness of Canadians to take advantage of the enormous opportunities this agreement presents us with; opportunities that will open up within the U.S. market, and opportunities that will present themselves in the markets of the world.

The status quo is not the answer in our relationship with the U.S., nor in our relationships with the trading nations of the world. I support this agreement and the Canadian Chamber of Commerce supports this agreement, because we share in the business community's enthusiasm and have confidence in their ability to compete effectively.

The dawn of a new tomorrow awaits those with the optimism and vision to make this country of ours a more secure, prosperous, and exciting place to live.

Chapter six:
stepping out from
behind the tariff wall

J.E. Newall

Mr. Newall is chairman, president and chief executive officer, Dupont Canada Inc. From an address to the Business Strategies and Free Trade Conference sponsored by The C.D. Howe Institute and the Faculty of Management, University of Toronto, in Toronto January 26, 1988.

Until the early or mid 1970's our company had a strategy of investing primarily to serve Canadian markets and using the tariff to shield us from competition. Despite that, we consistently delivered substantial export sales as well. We believed high tariffs were the birthright of Canadian manufacturers.

I thought that those federal and provincial policy advisors who where constantly preaching the benefits of free trade and lower tariffs were misinformed. I thought they were out of touch, impractical and theoretical idealists who should be locked up somewhere before they did irreparable harm to the manufacturing sector. Every now and then, when I run into my friend Jean Chrétien, he delights in reminding me that he knew me when I was a protectionist. He always manages to say it so it sounds like an unmentionable social disease.

About 10 or 12 years ago we, at Du Pont Canada, came to the reluctant conclusion that all those people who believed in liberalizing trade or reducing tariffs seemed to be winning the policy debate. Furthermore, when we looked back, it was apparent that the trend to lower tariffs had been underway since the late thirties. Almost 40 years. You might be pardoned for concluding I was a slow learner. In self-defense all I can say is that I had lots of company.

So we made a pivotal decision. We decided we were out of step — not the rest of the parade. We established a key guideline — we would make only major investments in businesses which were already fully competitive internationally in costs, quality and product performance, or which were on a path to get to that position soon. We would strongly support only those businesses that were or could become equal to or better than the best. By and large we have stuck with this policy.

Today, more than 85 percent of our sales revenue and more than 90 percent of our earnings come from businesses with very strong competitive positions. Those strong competitive positions were delivered in part by the continuous and exceptionally successful efforts of our employees. They raised productivity at well above average rates. I am very proud of their outstanding accomplishments. Business excellence and people excellence are inseparable.

Eight or 10 years ago an immediate move to zero tariffs would have caused us great difficulty. As a result of our pivotal decision, today it would not. And, since the tariff cuts are being phased in over five to 10 years, we have ample time to use our ingenuity to resolve whatever problems we haven't licked so far.

The move to eliminate tariffs creates a great many opportunities that are not present, even in a relatively low tariff environment. That is especially the case since the new treaty is coupled with arrangements that reduce the ability of U.S. companies to employ their countervail and anti-dumping safeguard measures to harass Canadian suppliers.

Simply put, with the trade agreement it is now a safe strategy to invest in Canada to serve North America. Previously, except for those businesses covered by the auto pact and resource industries, that strategy could be questioned.

Our company serves a great many different Canadian market segments with many different products and services. Each will respond to the new trade opportunity uniquely.

Our most important strategy change is specialization. It will be much easier for our businesses to make what they can produce best for specialized market niches for the full North American market. Many of our businesses have been pursuing this strategy to some degree or other already.

However, hurdling tariffs into the U.S. of five, 10 or 15 percent makes a big dint in your profit margin. It also often puts you at a critical cost disadvantage versus U.S. producers, especially in periods of excess capacity when competition is intense. In such periods in Canada we've often ducked down behind the tariff, and stolen market share from foreign producers. They do the same to us in export markets. Eliminating the tariff will put us on a more equal footing with U.S.-based producers and give us more confidence to defend out market positions through thick and thin.

I believe Canadian-based manufacturers have some inherent advantages that are often overlooked. An order that is a short run to a U.S. producer is often a golden profit opportunity for a Canadian. Circumstances have forced Canadian manufacturers to become experts in producing short runs efficiently. I believe Canadian manufacturers are far better at this than most producers in the U.S.A., where scale has tended to receive priority over flexibility. Our friends in Du Pont, south of the border, often enthuse over our ability in Canada to achieve both flexibility and cost competitiveness. We, at Du Pont Canada, believe that the strategy of seeking out and serving specialized market niches on a North American basis has great potential for us.

In some areas, we will pursue a production rationalization strategy in concert with Du Pont plants south of the border, thus making operations in both countries more efficient and more competitive. Some of this has already been done, but often the tariffs more than offset the savings.

At Du Pont Canada, our response to the free trade agreement is being governed by the following considerations:

•The U.S. market is not only a large market, it is also a very rich market. It supports an extraordinary diversity of consumer taste and it is flexible and fast moving. It welcomes and adopts new products or services easily and quickly. For entrepreneurial and innovative Canadian companies, that is a definition of heaven.

•We will pursue a wide variety of different business strategies in response to the new opportunity. Market niche specialization and product rationalization will be among those strategies. We are confident they will work because we are already on that path in many areas. Many Canadian companies may have a natural advantage with the specialization strategy.

•Much of our competition in the Canadian and U. S. markets stems from offshore producers. That competition will continue. However, by removing the tariffs North/South we are giving each other a leg up in each other's markets. And, we are improving our competitive position relative to the offshore producers. That is why some other countries are expressing concern. This pact benefits North American producers partly at the expense of offshore competitors.

•The combination of the elimination of tariffs and putting the rule of law back into the U.S. countervail and anti-dump makes Canada a more attractive place to invest to serve the North American market.

•The U.S. has a very attractive investment climate, but so does Canada. The quality of life in Canada ranks with the best in the world. The additional wealth created by this trade pact will be a big help in providing funds to maintain and improve our excellent social safety net and our health and educational system. The biggest risk faced by our high quality social support systems is not free trade. It is the potential of a continuing crisis in funding caused by inadequate wealth generation.

•We've had almost 40 years of tariff cuts and through it all our economy has progressed. It's hard to visualize why removing the last quarter of the tariffs would create great hardship when removal of the first three quarters helped create prosperity.

Canadian manufacturers can compete successfully. In fact they are doing so today. At Du Pont Canada, we are eager for its implementation. The sooner we get on with this trade arrangement the better-for Canada -- and for the U.S.

Chapter seven:
truck and trade with the Yankees

Thomas d'Aquino

Mr. d'Aquino is president and chief executive officer of the Business Council on National Issues. From an address to a conference on Canadian-American free trade at McGill University, Montreal, March 19, 1987.

We don't always appreciate the critical link between trade and the growth of jobs. Since the Second World War, the value of our exports has increased more than 12-fold. During this period we achieved extraordinary economic growth at the same time that barriers to trade were being lowered throughout the industrialized world. Exports have built our nation. Exports have provided us with one of the highest standards of living in the world.

By no means is Canada the only beneficiary of four decades of trade liberalization. Other industrialized countries have seen huge increases in real income as well. And just as significantly, hundreds of millions of people in less-developed countries have benefited from their products gaining freer access to the markets of industrialized countries. In the post-war world, trade liberalization became a powerful engine of growth, jobs, and opportunity. This period has been referred to as the "most dynamic single generation of wide-spread growth in human history" — a time when the world's annual output of goods and services tripled.

What was the world like before this global move towards trade liberalization? It was a time when the protectionists held sway, when beggar-thy-neighbor policies were commonplace. It was a time of world depression, of massive unemployment, of hunger and misery. In Canada, the election of 1930 brought to power the Bennett government on the platform of "Canada First." In the United States, the Congress passed the Hawley-Smoot legislation which raised tariffs on U.S. imports to prohibitive levels. By 1933, Canadian exports to the United States had fallen to one-third the 1929 level and imports had fallen to one-quarter. The hard lessons of the thirties should have taught us a great deal — most importantly that blind protectionism is a dead-end street. To give into it is to accept inevitable economic impoverishment and, in time, moral impoverishment as well.

What does a free trade agreement mean?

Today, trade liberalization remains a dominant imperative of the global agenda, and the Canadian government and the Canadian business community remain vigorous proponents of the dismantling of trade barriers at the multilateral level. But since the early 1980s, we in the Business Council on National Issues have also advocated the conclusion of a comprehensive free trade agreement between Canada and the United States.

Let me be perfectly clear about what we mean by a "free trade agreement." I am talking about a legal undertaking between the two nations that accords with the provisions of the General Agreement on Tariffs and Trade (GATT). The GATT defines a free trade area as one in which the barriers would be removed from "substantially all the trade" between parties to the agreement.

In opting for such an arrangement with the United States, the Business Council rejects both a bilateral customs union or a common market. A customs union, in our view, goes too far. It would provide for unrestricted movement of goods and services between Canada and the United States, and for common tariffs and other trade barriers against third countries. A common market goes even further. It would add to the features of a customs union the free movement of labor and capital between the two countries.

I want to dispel a myth commonly associated with the free trade idea by our critics — the belief that a free trade agreement leads to a rapid dismantling of all barriers to trade. This is not the case. The full terms of a free trade agreement are usually implemented over time, with transitional arrangements for some industries and with adjustments for affected workers. Even in its advanced stage, a free trade association might still permit some degree of so-called "managed trade." Free trade is not a black or white issue, as some would have us believe.

An agreement will reduce Canada's vulnerability

Recent experience has taught us that in the absence of a formal agreement, we in Canada are seriously vulnerable to American protectionist actions aimed directly at us. What better examples can I offer than the cases of shakes and shingles and softwood lumber? In recent years, quotas, surcharges, anti-dumping, and countervailing duties have in one way or another affected more than $6 billion of Canadian exports to the United States. The industries threatened provide close to 150,000 jobs. But we are also being hurt by American protectionist actions aimed at others. Consider the serious damage to Canadian wheat farmers that has resulted from disputes between the United States and the European Community.

Yes, we are enormously vulnerable to United States protectionism, and an agreement would reduce that vulnerability. But support for the federal government's trade initiative among Canada's business leaders is not based simply on fear that access to the American market will be curtailed. This support has a positive dimension, and this perspective has not received the attention in the current debate that it deserves.

First, because of the difference in the size of the two countries, free trade holds out the promise of providing greater benefits to Canada than to the United States. The U.S. economy is about 10 times bigger than ours. Free access to it opens up vast opportunities. For example: an increase of just one percent in Canada's share of the government procurement market in the United States — a $750 billion market that is now largely closed to us — would result in some some 75,000 new jobs in this country. And this is the tip of the iceberg. The predominant view among economists who have studied the costs and benefits of bilateral free trade is that Canada's gross national product would rise by three to eight percent. This consensus is supported by the findings of the Macdonald Royal Commission.

Second, improved access to the huge United States market of some 250 million people will help us come to grips with the problems that threaten our competitiveness. It would encourage larger, lower-cost production in our factories. It will help us address one of the worst productivity records in the industrialized world by making our industries more specialized and more efficient. It would strengthen our capacity to compete in our own market, in the United States, and particularly in the highly competitive global marketplace.

We would see the benefits of this improved competitiveness in very concrete ways. The prices of many of the things that we buy would fall. The incomes of Canadian households would rise. So would consumer spending and investment. In the wake of all this, jobs would grow. As a nation, we would have a better chance of remaining among the world's leading economic powers.

The third reason why Canadian business leaders favor freer trade with the Americans is that it would make Canada a more attractive place to invest — more attractive to Canadians themselves, and to foreign investors as well. I have spoken to many in the United States, Europe, and Japan who see secure access to the United States market under the umbrella of a comprehensive trade agreement as an alluring prospect. As things stand now, a combination of tariffs, other barriers to trade, a fear of growing protectionism in the United States, and the lingering effects of nationalist policies in our own country, have driven a great deal of investment away from Canada. This has cost us dearly in lost opportunities.

There is another reason why Canada's business leaders favor freer trade with the Americans. A bilateral trade pact would help address one of the most frustrating economic problems we face — a problem that the protectionists appear little concerned about. I refer to the barriers to free trade that we Canadians have erected against one another in our own country, barriers that have impeded the free movement of goods, labor and capital among the 10 provinces, barriers that have fragmented our already small domestic market and made us less competitive internationally.

I want to make two points very clear. Some critics are saying that in advocating a trade pact with the United States, the federal government and the business community are turning their backs on efforts to achieve world trade liberalization. Nothing is further from the truth. Government and business leaders alike strongly support the new round of multilateral negotiations launched at Punta del Este, Uruguay, and for good reason. At stake is more than $2.6 trillion in annual world exports of goods and $800-900 billion in services, and the need to restore order to a world trading system dangerously close to disintegration.

In fact, a Canada-United States agreement could further the goals of multilateral trade liberalization in some very significant ways. The agreement could embrace accords in areas such as services, intellectual property, and investment — accords which to date have largely eluded multilateral negotiators. It could provide a model to the 92 nations who subscribe to the General Agreement on Tariffs and Trade (GATT) on how to strengthen dispute-resolution mechanisms and on how to improve the existing codes on subsidies and government procurement.

My second point concerns third markets. Our interest in reaching an accord with the Americans should not be interpreted as a willingness on our part to forsake other markets. The European Community is the world's largest market and offers Canada some attractive prospects in the long term. So do the fast-growing markets of the Pacific basin. Furthermore, Canada's business leaders believe that a stronger Canada in North America will magnify Canada's ability to compete in the global marketplace. Recently a Japanese businessman expressed this fact to me in his own words. "If Canada can't make it in North American," he said, "it will never make it in the world at large."

Canadian sovereignty is not at stake

But would we lose our political independence? Would our culture and our "Canadian way of life" gradually disappear? Would Canadian unity diminish? In my view, these things will never happen.

Here is why.

First, the Canadian and American economies are already highly integrated. A great deal of the trade that passes between the two countries is already free. And yet would any well-informed Canadian argue that we are less independent now than in the days of high tariffs? Can a case be made that we have a weaker sense of national identity now than, say, 30 years ago? I do not believe so. Will a comprehensive trade pact that results in the incremental disman-

> ## *Clear minds, dispassionate enquiry, and intellectual honesty is what this great debate needs*

tling of remaining tariffs and other barriers to trade erode our deeply rooted commitment to Canada? I cannot see why.

Second, the protectionists argue that free trade today will lead before long to a common market, and eventually to a Canada-United States political union. This argument has no foundation. In this century there is not a single example where a high level of trade liberalization between two countries led to political integration. And furthermore, there is no significant support in either Canada or the United States for a common market or a political union.

If the protectionists are confused, let's not let them confuse us or the issue. The arrangement being proposed between Canada and the United States is not new. It has been tried many times, and successfully. It is close in character to the trade accords negotiated in the 1970s among members of the European Free Trade Association (EFTA), and between a number of western European countries and the European community. More recently the Australians and New Zealanders have concluded a free trade agreement. These accords aim to liberalize trade and provide more stable market access. They do not embrace the objective of economic integration, and there is not the slightest evidence that these agreements have eroded the political independence or the sovereignty of the countries that have signed them.

Culture is a special case

A discussion of political independence and sovereignty in Canada these days inevitably leads to the sensitive issue of culture. Many Canadians are genuinely worried that our culture industries — those engaged in periodical and book publishing, records, film, and video — could not survive in a free trade environment. This subject provokes strong emotions on both sides of the border — witness the conflict in the mid-1970s surrounding the non-deductability of advertising placed in foreign media, or the recent dispute surrounding Gulf+Western's acquisition of the Prentice-Hall book publishing company.

I share this concern. I believe that some Canadian companies in the cultural sector would be put at a substantial disadvantage by a combination of free trade and the elimination of present investment regulations which limit the right of foreign companies to establish themselves in cultural industries. With other products, Canadian companies can carve out niches and compete against their American counterparts. Canadian cultural products are not exportable in the same way. Many of them will have meaning only to us, so we can never hope to overcome American economies of scale in this area.

Why do Canadians make the linkage between cultural industries on the one hand, and the sovereignty question on the other? Why has this issue become so explosive? If you understand this issue, then to a large extent you have fathomed the psyche of Canadians. Consciously and unconsciously, we value and depend on the indigenous vehicles which express who we are as a people — whether through the pages of newspapers or books, the sound of records, or the images of film. To the extent that trade liberalization threatens their existence in Canadian hands, this will be seen as a menace to our independence as a people.

It was our awareness and sensitivity to this issue that prompted the Business Council, in testimony before Canadian parliamentarians more than a year ago, to argue that "care must be taken to protect the sensitive sectors that are essential to the maintenance of Canada's political and cultural values... and where necessary, foreign investment and competition in the cultural sector should be controlled to ensure that this important area of our national life is not sacrificed in the quest for a more competitive Canadian economy."

The debate in Canada about our future economic relations with the United States is far too important to jobs, growth, and our future prosperity to have it become the subject of a titanic partisan struggle. Clear minds, dispassionate enquiry, and intellectual honesty is what this great debate needs. And this is what the people of Canada must demand of all those who are seeking to shape its outcome.

Chapter eight:
productivity and free trade

David Daubney, MP

Mr. Daubney is chairman of the House of Commons Standing Committee on Justice, and Solicitor General. From an address to the Ottawa West Rotary Club, Ottawa, September 8, 1987.

Once we accepted the premise that the deficit had to be reduced, we had to take steps to increase the total wealth of Canada. We had to create conditions for economic growth, so that rather than just tinkering with redistribution of existing national wealth, new wealth could be created. We have succeeded in doing this to a very limited extent. Canada's economy is growing again. That is why unemployment is coming down, why government revenues are increasing, as the income of the people increases, and why the deficit is being reduced.

To make substantial progress, however, to effectively eliminate unemployment, to give Canadians the growth in real income which they want, and at the same time to increase government program delivery, we need a dramatic improvement in Canadian productivity.

Improvements in productivity brought us the surplus which transformed the Western world from agrarian to industrial and then to post-industrial society. In our periods of most rapid productivity growth, government services and our personal wealth increased the most rapidly. Since 1973, a period which coincides with the growth in the Canadian deficit from zero to the current levels, Canadian productivity grew very slowly The result included a sharp jump in unemployment; increased levels of poverty, specifically in the regions; slow growth in personal income, and growing pessimism about our ability to compete with the rest of the world.

If Canada is to increase its national wealth, we need to go beyond our own borders, to sell our services and our products to the rest of the world, and to make a profit on the deal. Canadian business cannot, with our small population and fragmented domestic market, grow quickly enough to create the new wealth we need as a nation.

Because our markets are small, per capita production in Canada has not matched the United States. American industry can afford to specialize and invest in huge production runs. By the nature and size of our domestic markets, Canadian productivity begins with a disadvantage, and that is why our output per worker has traditionally been lower than in the United States.

We have been improving our position in comparison with the Americans. In 1965 our productivity was 75 percent of the American rate; by last year it was 91 percent. But it would have been much better, had we not faced substantial productivity problems in the period of 1980-86.

Between 1980 and 1986, American productivity improved faster than ours, at least in part because the American dollar increased in value by 50 percent. American products became more expensive, and American industry had to produce more at lower costs to make its products saleable internationally. Canadian productivity in the same period, increased slowly.

Our problem has been productivity in our manufacturing sector. Our primary industries, resource extraction and farming, as well as our construction and service industries, have performed well. But our manufacturing industries, most located in Quebec and Ontario, performed sluggishly. Canadian manufacturers were 18 percent behind their American competition in output per worker in 1980, and 26 percent behind them in 1986. In 1985 our per capita productivity increased by only six tenths of one percent.

But there is good news here. Our economic policies are working, and by last year our productivity began to increase, rising by 2.3 percent. That is why unemployment is dropping, and why personal income is rising. One 1986 study of the 22 OECD countries -- United States, Canada, Western Europe, Japan -- indicated that Canadian productivity jumped sharply, rising from 10th place in 1985 to second place in 1986.

Where it was very important, we fared well. Canada was third lowest in levels of unit labor costs in manufacturing, because we were strong in things like employee absences from work. We were first, you might be interested to know, in having the fewest number of paid annual days of leave per skilled employee, ninth out of 22 in absenteeism, and 13th in length of the work week. We gained strongly, too, because our inflation rates dropped.

Can government increase productivity? Yes, it can. It will not do it, however, and the record is clear on this, by coddling Canadian industry, by providing it with endless protection against the reality of world competition. Canadian workers are productive, but Canadian managers are unimaginative and cautious, turning to government for protection at every ripple in the international economic system. Canadian manufacturing managers in the past have seen threats where they should have seen challenges.

The Canadian government reacted to the oil price rises in the 1970's not by letting this price rise drive industry into cost-cutting innovations, but by regulating and subsidizing oil prices. The result was strangulation of a legitimately productive resource extraction industry, and stagnation in the complacent eastern Canadian manufacturing sector.

There are things government can do to improve Canadian economic performance, and our chances of creating new wealth. Free trade is one opportunity — only an opportunity, not a guaranteed sure thing — for Canadian industry to improve its productivity. Our productivity is nine percent behind the American level, and with sound economic management, is once again closing in on the American levels. And this is even given the fact that we have a domestic market one-tenth the size of the American market. If we had unrestricted access to the American market, making use of the same economies of scale which had given Americans their advantage over us in the past, the best of our companies would do much better. There is good reason to believe that our productivity, and our per capita wealth, would exceed the American levels.

It is clear, and this is one problem for the Americans, that we stand to gain much more than they do from free trade. Americans provide 78 percent of our trading market. We provide 18 percent of theirs. They stand to increase their market access size by about 10 percent, by another 25 million people. That is not bad, but it is nowhere near the one thousand percent increase in Canadian market access. We would have an additional 250 million people to sell to.

Of course American industry is used to producing at those levels, and would face little problem in extending production runs by 10 percent. The weakest of our industries, those which have been protected for decade after decade from international competition, industries such as textiles and footwear which have promised increased productivity, if protection were extended, and have never fulfilled those promises, would face tough times indeed. The best of our industries, those with a track record of innovative management and investment in productivity, would prosper, grabbing huge new markets, and creating jobs in the process.

Free trade would mean fewer subsidies from government, but a requirement for government to provide the infrastructure to encourage an increase in quality and productivity. Canada would have to provide, in short, the best education and research facilities in the world. There can be no shrinking from this investment. If free trade is implemented, and to the extent that it is implemented, federal and provincial governments will be forced to invest more heavily in research and development, in universities and in worker retraining and resettlement.

The money can be found. Our current tariffs are costing Canadian consumers between five and seven billion dollars a year in elevated prices.This is money which must be used to ease the transition to new and more productive jobs, in companies and in industrial sectors which are competitive. We have to make the transition from unstable industries which produce jobs only so long as they are protected, to industries which provide real jobs based on strong productivity.

It has been estimated that the information industries, those activities in which the production, consumption or transformation of information, or the production of machines which help us perform these tasks, are now the largest group of industries in the world. One estimate is that annual world-wide turnover of the information industries may reach two trillion dollars within the next three years.

There are few important Canadian industries — farming, fishing, trapping and a few others excepted — where there is not now a substantial information component to the economic value produced.

As many as half of all Canadian workers may now be employed in information industries. Finance, real estate and insurance industries, government at all levels, the massive service sector, all make significant use of information. Even in the manufacturing sector, sales market research and management deal primarily with information, and computerized production techniques have increased the proportion of information workers in production processes.

What is significant here is the economic **value added** to individual work and to society through the production, distribution, and analysis of information. What policy makers should remember is that actual employment in the infrastructure-producing high technology industries may be the least important economic component of this information work. The identification and exploitation of resources and markets, the development of new products and services can transform the viability of traditional industries. The failure to make use of new information and techniques can render such industries uncompetitive with foreign firms which are using information intelligently. When this happens, or when technology is used improperly, it is a failure of management, not of technology.

The fact is that management in an information age and a free trade economy, will have to move fast, and creatively. It will be required to make intelligent, tough decisions to force productivity increases. What is surprising to a lot of people is that managers should have to be forced, by the prospect of something like free trade, into strategies which will increase productivity. The Science Council of Canada produced a report a few weeks ago, which suggested that one particular industry, forestry, do the following things:

•Develop more sophisticated and better designed products to meet consumer and industrial applications.

•Become more committed to delivery of quality products targeted to customer needs.

66

•Make technological excellence a top priority.

There were a number of other recommendations as well, but what was striking was that any managers should have to be told to seek excellence, or to learn what their customers want.

Canadian companies have to invest in technological renovation to increase productivity. Some are doing this very well. American Motors of Canada has invested $700 million upgrading its assembly plant in Bramalea and Dofasco has invested another $700 million on

> *We can whimper in the corner of world trade, bemoaning our second-rate status, or we can take responsibility for our future by competing with the world's best*

its plant in Hamilton. General Motors has invested billions in new technology in Oshawa. Smaller companies like Champion Road Machinery Limited of Goderich, Ontario are investing millions in new technology — all to improve their productivity. But if these companies are rewarded with high productivity, it will not be simply because they bought it with new technology. The new technologies of robotics, word processing or computer-aided design are expensive, and if improperly implemented, will not pay for themselves.

Studies of the implementation of innovations in complex organizations show clearly that the **process** of implementation — **how** workers are involved in decisions about purchases of new equipment, and how to implement it — is essential to innovation success.

The technological quick-fix is a chimera. Computer-aided design systems have been touted as producing increases in labor productivity of up to 6,000 percent. The reality is much different. When the systems are implemented, productivity increases an average of 50 percent — not bad, but not enough to justify the huge capital investments in the new technology.

But these expenses can be justified if productivity is seen as more than just reducing costs of labor, or increasing profits. Increased productivity can be taken in higher profits, in higher wages, in lower prices, or in better quality of products at a constant price.

In Canada, too often, productivity improvements have been channelled to profit or salary increases, rather than attention to customer satisfaction through higher quality and lower prices.

Japan has more than doubled its output per hour over the last ten years. During this same period, real wages have risen only 20 to 25 percent. Customers have benefited through lower costs and higher quality of products. Japan, as a result, has expanded and entrenched its share of global markets, and its prospects for job security.

In Canada, over the same period, what productivity gains there have been, have been paid out not to customers but to workers or shareholders.

Successful management is management which is wedded primarily to customer satisfaction. Robert Ferchat, the president of Northern Telecom, one of our most successful and innovative companies, estimates that 80 percent of his company's revenues come from products and systems which did not exist seven years ago. Northern Telecom's successes are the product of skilled and innovative managers, making intelligent decisions about what scientists and engineers should be working on.

So, some Canadian industries will compete, and will make good use of the new market access which free trade will bring. Others will not. Poor management will fail.

Some critics of free trade in the Liberal and New Democratic parties fear that Canadian industry would become too dependent on American markets. This ignores the fact that we are already dependent on them, and our other trading partners, for our economic survival. But right now, our dependence is one of fear, not of opportunity.

We fear protectionism, tariffs and subsidies which Americans and Europeans use to maintain artificially low commodity prices. Sixty three Canadian industries are subsidized in one form or another, through cash grants, tax breaks, tax credits, low interest loans, loan guarantees or regulated prices which keep costs artificially low. Americans subsidize 35 industries.

Canadian industry is protected by tariffs which are higher than those which protect American industry, 50 to 100 percent higher in many cases. Knitting mills in Canada are protected by a 21.5 percent tariff — versus a 12.6 percent tariff in the U.S. Canadian clothing tariffs are 17 percent, and American tariffs on clothes are a little less then 11 percent.

But Americans have a significantly higher number of non-tariff barriers to deter foreign imports, and in the last two years we have seen American trade action against hogs, fish, lumber, steel products, footwear, beef, sugars and syrups and a number of other Canadian products. Over six billion dollars in Canadian exports have been affected negatively by these actions. Between 1980 and 1986 the Americans undertook 22 antidumping actions, 14 countervailing duty cases, and six escape clause actions against Canadian manufacturers.

We are dependent on our trading partners, and vulnerable to their moods but Americans bear us no ill will. The Gallup organization did a study for the Chicago Council on Foreign Relations last year, and found that Canada rated first in the world in the warmth of feeling Americans feel for other countries. But they face daily pressures from their own industry, to protect themselves. What we have to do is take advantage of the good will they have for us, to come to agreements with the Americans and others to solidify our access to their markets. We are continuing to pursue multilateral negotiations with the 91 other members of GATT in the eighth round of tariff reduction negotiations. But 91 negotiating partners are hard to deal with. If we are going to reach a deal with anybody, it will be with the Americans, first.

One significant benefit of a free trade agreement would be the elimination of a host of insidious and ridiculous barriers to free trade within Canada, between provinces. Right now we are making more progress on the elimination of international trade barriers than on interprovincial trade barriers.

In 1985 the city of Aylmer had to rip up its sidewalks because Ontario bricks had been used in construction. Moosehead ale from Nova Scotia and milk from Quebec could not be sold in Ontario, and a number of provinces had buy-provincial regulations which discriminated against products from other parts of Canada.

It is amazing that Canadian industry has any kind of productivity improvement at all with this small-minded provincial attitude at work in our own province and across the country.

I am tired of the hyperbole on both sides of this issue. Free trade is no panacea for our economic ills. Free trade will provide us with the **opportunity** to improve our productivity, and with it our national wealth. But this is **just** an opportunity, **not** a guarantee.

There is no magic, white or black, in free trade. Taken alone, it will not break our independence or make our fortune. It is one tool, one approach which offers us new roads for exploration, where old paths have proven rocky and rough, sometimes dead ends. It is up to us to make free trade work, and that means we will need lean, innovative industries.

I see free trade as much a tool for national unity as bilingualism, the national railroad or a constitution. The poorest of Canada's regions stand to gain the most from free trade, but the indications are that on balance, with creative management, we will all profit.

There are no free rides, no sure things, but there are intelligent trade-offs, and this is one deal we should make.

We can hide from the opportunity, but if we do, we will remain a minor league economic power, with minor league incomes and a major league national debt. We can whimper in the corner of world trade, bemoaning our second-rate status, or we can take responsibility for our future, by competing on the world's terms, with the best the world has to offer.

Chapter nine:
billions and billions
from oil and gas

Arne Nielson

Mr. Nielson is chairman of the Canadian Petroleum Association's task force on free trade. From a presentation to the House of Commons committee on external affairs and international trade, Edmonton, November 24, 1987.

A free trade agreement with the world's major market for petroleum and its products is welcomed by members of the Canadian Petroleum Association. Free trade is a logical extension of the energy policies that have been developed over the last three years. It is consistent with the deregulation of oil prices, competitive flow of oil imports and exports, and the changes to the natural gas regime.

With the freest possible bilateral trade in energy between Canada and the United States, Canada will be exempt from U.S. protectionist measures that might otherwise be contemplated. There is talk in the United States about a levy on oil imports, and of an import tariff on Canadian natural gas. Such moves would have a very negative effect on our industry. A free trade agreement would protect us from them. U.S. markets are critically important to the development of Canada's oil and gas resources. Canada has in the past derived tremendous benefit from those markets , and continues to, because of the economic activity, employment opportunities, and technological advances which those sales generate. For example, net export revenues from crude oil, natural gas, and its by-products to the United States — $5 billion for the first eight months of this year — were more than Canada's total trade surplus of $4.3 billion.

It is our assessment that without those export sales, investment spending by our sector might have been some $30 billion lower during the last 10 years. In future, development of heavy oil, natural gas, and frontier production for the benefit of Canadians will equally depend on the availability of U.S. markets. Export markets provide an outlet for surplus natural gas production and for much of the heavy oil we produce. Export markets will be needed to bring into production large scale frontier developments. Not only will much wealth be generated from these projects, but continuity of supply to Canadians will be enhanced by their development, facilitated by access to export markets.

Certain concerns have been raised regarding the energy provisions in the agreement. Let me briefly deal with some of them. We in Canada have followed a very protectionist policy, but this policy, in the long term, did not truly provide the expected security of gas supply. The reality is that regulation or export restriction has nothing to do with security of supply. Quite the contrary. The requirement for holding 25 years of reserves before permitting exports reduced the incentive to develop gas. It is very costly to hold reserves unnecessarily in the ground, a cost that must ultimately be borne by the users of natural gas.

Let me illustrate that point. In 1971 the National Energy Board determined that no surplus of natural gas would remain after due allowance had been made for the reasonably foreseeable Canadian requirements. As a result, we lost sales opportunities. This was quite unnecessary. The remaining gas reserves, at the end of 1971, were 62.5 trillion cubic feet in western Canada. After producing 37.5 trillion cubic feet in the interim our reserves have grown to about 74 trillion cubic feet. This expansion occurred thanks to rising price expectations, not to our export policies.

The point I wish to make is that reserves at any time are only a shelf-ready inventory, depleted at one end and replenished at the other. What really counts is the investment number, not the shelf-inventory number. Holding gas in the ground discourages investment.

Let me mention three more reasons. Our exploration effort is unpredictable. We have difficulty predicting the size of a discovery and thus the available output, unlike a manufacturing facility that can be designed for a specific production. The economics of scale also play a major role in our business. For an offshore project or an oil sands plant to be economic, a certain size is required. The economics dictate as well that the output from such projects be as close to capacity as possible, which in turn requires unconstrained market access.

Second, when we consider the industry's history, we find significant capacity under-utilization because of market constraints, often politically induced. With today's lower price expectations, we need to ensure greater cost effectiveness. Market access is essential if we are to operate closer to capacity. Unit costs fall when production facilities and pipelines operate full.

A third very important benefit for a free trade agreement is the improved confidence that will be engendered in trading relationships. This will allow Canadian production to expand with greater certainty. It will also allow Canadian exports to compete on a more equal footing in the U.S. market. This will mean both increased sales and more competitive prices as Canadian production moves away from meeting just supplementary demands in the United States market.

Aside from the immediate benefits to our industry of having assured access to the large and expanding U.S. market, there are indirect benefits. Our industry provides the feedstock for much of Canada's petrochemical industry. That industry should grow once tariff restrictions are removed. Canadian methanol presently faces an 18 percent U.S. duty, and polyethylene a 12.5 percent duty. Removal of those impediments to export sales should offer not only a welcome boost to the petrochemical industry but a major market increase for Canadian petroleum production at home.

Economic evidence across the nation confirms our industry's claim that activity in many other sectors of our economy is stimulated by activity in Canada's petroleum industry. When activity is strong, benefits in the form of jobs, taxes, demand for equipment and services, and economic activity flow to all parts of Canada.

The first activity takes place in financial areas when a project is launched. It flows from there to construction, to the wholesale and manufacturing sectors, and then to retail sales. A review of shopping lists from just a small sample of our members operating from western Canada reveals that more than 4,500 Ontario firms provide goods and services to the industry. Central Canada is our industry's supermarket, manufacturing and marketing much of the wide assortment of industrial and consumer goods used by the industry and its people.

Aside from thousands of kilometres of pipe, the industry uses train-loads of cement, valves, electric motors, meters, gauges, computers, helicopters, telephones, telemetering and telemonitoring equipment, trucks and cars, dragline shovels, wheelbarrows, steel cable, chain and virtually any other goods manufactured in Canada.

Chapter ten:
the envy of the world

Bernard Landry

Mr. Landry is professor of economics, University of Quebec in Montreal, and former Quebec minister for international trade. From a submission to the House of Commons standing committee on external affairs and international trade, Montreal, November 17, 1987.

The first point I want to make is that this 35-page agreement drawn up by the Canadian and American negotiators is the envy of almost all Western countries. I do not think that has been stressed enough. The main client of most countries in the world, both in the East and the West, is the United States of America. This is true of the Federal Republic of Germany as well as Japan, France and Italy. They have to make do with multilateral negotiations. They all have to sit down at the GATT table. The EEC countries must first get together for negotiations among themselves and settle their own business before dealing with the United States of America in Geneva or wherever the GATT negotiations are taking place.

Here we have the United States' main trading partner, Canada, managing to obtain an agreement that establishes its particular position. Out of all the countries in the world it is the one that trades most and is the most closely linked economically with the United States, and here we have that status taking a legal form.

In the past few months I have had the occasion to discuss this agreement with a number of foreigners, who expressed great admiration for the team of Canadian negotiators and for the Canadian government's exploit, particularly in a climate of mounting protectionism.

It is true that a free trade arrangement was almost concluded under Mackenzie King, but for some obscure reason it did not come to pass. Some historians claim, tongue in cheek, that he communicated with the spirit of Sir Wilfrid Laurier who told him to stay away from it or he would lose the election.

I do not think that is the case, but it was a lot easier at the time to talk about free trade with the United States. It was in the period of generosity following the war and the time when the GATT and the UN came into existence. Those days are over; as was said by someone who does not at all share my views on the matter, we are now in the period of Rambonomics, to use the expression coined by the French minister to describe the attitude displayed by the Americans for the past several months.

That is my first point. The agreement is the envy of other nations.

Turning to my second point, I refer to my personal experience. As Quebec Minister of International Trade, with my colleague from British Columbia and several federal colleagues, I was involved in the first softwood lumber case. Like most economists, I have always been theoretically in favor of free trade. For economists free trade is a motherhood issue. But after having to go to Washington three times and literally crawl before the people in the American departments... to scrape by and finally win our first lumber case... this was when I became keenly aware of the dangers of the status quo. For the elected representatives of a great sovereign state like Canada and its components with their significant degree of autonomy to be subject to American legislation, before an American tribunal, using American criteria, and have Washington treat them like any other North American lobby group, is just not acceptable. On this particular occasion it was brought home to us because we were the targets. There are other situations where we have found ourselves on the receiving end, though it was not intended. In the case of softwood lumber, they were aiming at us and they got us.

In a recent dispute with the European Economic Community they threatened a 200 percent increase in the duty on white wine, cognac and cheese because membership of Portugal and Spain in the Community meant that Americans could no longer sell and avoid the common external tariff. But because of our GATT commitments and the principle of non-discrimination as well as the most favored nation clause, we would also have been hit by this 200 percent duty, like any Euoropean country. And of course, with a 200 percent duty, the only person in the United States eating Oka cheese would have been our Ambassador, Mr. Allan Gotlieb, whose diplomatic status would exempt him from paying the exorbitant duty.

So we have to beware of the status quo. The American economist who spoke to the committee a few weeks ago was probably too harsh in his terms in describing those who are against the agreement — I do think we have to conduct the debate in a civilized manner -- but there was very sharp criticism of those opposed to the agreement. It is a fact that such violent opposition to the agreement is a bit like playing with fire, under the circumstances. Because when they are aiming at us, they hit us and when they are not aiming at us, they hit us just the same. There are a few hundred protectionist measures before the American Congress which, whether they are intended for us or not, will surely affect us as the main trading partner of the United States of America.

The third point, and one that has probably been brought up

often, is the question of a large market. Our businesses are probably among the only ones in the western world that cannot count on guaranteed access to a domestic market of over 100 million inhabitants. I say practically the only ones because Australia and New Zealand, for geographical reasons, even with the Common Market they are setting up, will not constitute a market this size.

How can you expect our industry to be able to compete with northern Italy or Austria, or the Japanese or Americans, when all these countries have guaranteed access to a domestic market of hundreds of millions of consumers with money, whereas we in Quebec have a market of six million people, Quebec being part of the total Canadian market of 25 million, especially with the knowledge that the slightest protectionist threat, the smallest backward step, may compromise access to this market. The word "guaranteed" is therefore important.

As Quebec Minister of International Trade, I prospected the world's markets at the head of business delegations and I can tell you what our main problem is. It is a basic trade problem and it applies to Quebec as well as to Ontario and British Columbia. Our prices are not competitive. It is as simple as that. People do not buy our products because they like or dislike Canada, or because they like the red on our flag or the shape of the maple leaf; they look at the quality and the price. And why do you see so few Canadian consumer goods on the store shelves in different countries? It is because our quality in relation to price is not as good as our competitors', except on our own continent.

Reference was made a while ago to the failure of the third option. The third option was a very interesting proposition. I was much younger at the time and I was impressed by the attempts made by Mr. Jean-Luc Pepin during his Asian trips, etc. Now, I can see why there was not a third option. It is because our producers were not lucky enough to be up against large markets that would have forced them to meet the challenge of quality and lower prices, a challenge that turned other countries into formidable competitors.

You know that one of the big specialties in Quebec is consulting engineers. The export of grey matter. Three of the 10 largest engineering consulting firms in the world are in Montreal. Usually it is an activity with industrial spin-offs. If you are awarded the engineering contract, large industrial contracts come along with it. This is the case in Great Britain, in France, in Belgium and in Spain. It is not the case in Montreal. Why? Because although Lavallin's prices are competitive, the same is not true for the equipment that Lavallin could include in its specifications. So the industrial spin-offs from consulting engineer firms in Montreal are a mere shadow of what they should be and what they actually are in France, Italy and other countries.

Another point that has already been discussed this afternoon is our system of social measures. If my union friends had convinced me of their argument on social services and if my many progressive friends in Canada had convinced me that there was a threat to our Canadian system of social security, I would have immediately set aside all my convictions as a free-trader and all my experience based on economic problems. My experience and my background, as well

> ***When the Americans aim a protectionist blow at us, they hit us. When they are not aiming at us, they hit just the same.***

as the government to which I belonged, all make me very sensitive to social issues, yet I have never seen the slightest evidence that Canadian social measures would be threatened by a free trade agreement.

Such a claim does not stand up to rational analysis. Briefly, how would this rational analysis go? The American system is not nearly as good as ours and it is a lot more expensive. So why would we change ours to adapt to theirs when ours is less expensive and better? This question would have to be answered if it is claimed our social system is under threat. If anyone is to make adjustments, it would be the Americans. And depicting Americans as reactionaries without any social security at all is another extremist view, is it not?

There are progressive states in the United States with a progressive tradition and whose combined social measures can be compared to those found in Canada, whether it be Quebec, Ontario or any other province. ..Even in these states they envy the Canadian health system. Also, the fraction of the gross national product the United States devotes to health expenditures is higher than the corresponding fraction in Canada, and our system is better.

On the fourth point I have provided the rational arguments. For my progressive friends, some of them are here at the table. I would like to remind you that the example that fascinated progressives in English and French Canada, in Quebec and in Ontario, is Sweden. In my college days, if Sweden had not been there to give an example of the things we were dreaming of, we would have had to invent it. So what has been the development strategy of Sweden, probably the most advanced western country as far as social measures are concerned? It has always been free trade. Sweden is a founding member of the European Free Trade Association. It is still a member of the European Free Trade Association, which signed a free trade agreement with the European Economic Community at the time when Great Britain transferred from one association to the other. That means Volvos have guaranteed access to a market of over 355 million consumers with money in their pockets; the consumers of the European Economic Community as well as the European Free Trade Association. If any society can be cited for its advanced and generous social legislation, it is Sweden. Its strategy has never been based on putting up walls or on the fear of competition, but rather, the breaking down of barriers.

Fifth point: We often hear people say that they are in favor of free trade, but this particular agreement is poorly drafted, the proposal is a poor one. ... I say to the committee in all modesty that the text is a very good one if compared to free trade agreements signed by other countries and especially taking into account the pessimistic views held by certain segments of the population. Some people were claiming that the agreement would only be a face-saving device and that it would have no content. They said that a pretence would be made of concluding a free trade agreement, but that it would have no substance. But the substance is there. Mr. Simon Reisman, whom I do not have the pleasure of knowing, will go down in history, whether the agreement is ratified or not, as responsible for one of the best imaginable free trade agreements between two developed western countries. Let us hope that the lawyers will not do too much damage to this masterpiece bestowed on us by the economists and the negotiators.

Sixth and last point: it deals with something I have personal experience with. I am talking about nationalism. I am a Quebec nationalist, but that does not mean I am anti-Canadian. I have always believed that a Quebecer can be a Canadian, just as a Briton can be a European. The two do not rule each other out, they are not in conflict, and they never have been as far as I am concerned. As a Quebec nationalist, I am in a good position to speak to my friends who are Canadian nationalists and tell them that the most dangerous thing about the status quo is the possibility for this great power, probably the greatest in the history of humanity in all respects, to exercise undue influence on the destiny of the Canadian people in the absence of a treaty establishing the relationships between two countries. The softwood lumber case made me more aware than ever of the need for free trade, particularly because of its shocking implications for Canadian sovereignty.

American government inspectors came to my office in Quebec City to examine the business aid programs offered by the Government of Quebec. They were announced by my secretary in a way that made me think of the movies: "Sir, an inspector is here to see you."

I will never forget how fragile our institutions seemed to me in the absence of an agreement, setting forth our relationships with our huge neighbor.

You must have heard a hundred times about the mouse and the elephant or the horse and the rabbit. Every animal in creation has been brought in, as long as there is a big one and a small one. A small animal living near a large one had better have good relations with it. I think a free trade treaty is a good way to show the elephant that there is at least a fence. If it decides to sit on this fence, it will break it, but at least it will have been told that there is a fence and that there are orderly relations.

I will conclude by quoting one of the great minds of the French enlightenment, Lacordaire, who said that "in relations between the strong and the weak, freedom oppresses and law liberates. " In other words, between a very large power and a relatively small one — but not negligible, let us be clear on this, Canada is an important world power — it is better for relations to be orderly. The smaller of the two will have a greater chance of being respected.

Chapter eleven:
liberate the Maritimes

Gerald A. Regan

Mr. Regan is a former Premier of Nova Scotia and a former federal trade minister. From a submission to the House of Commons standing committee on external affairs and international trade.

I am fortunate to have the opportunity to appear to bear testament to the cause of free trade. It is a cause for which the Liberal Party, of which I have long been a member, has fought many battles. W.S. Field, who served as premier of Nova Scotia for 12 years and minister of finance of Canada for 15 years, Premier George Murray, and generations of Nova Scotian leaders fought for the principle that protective tariffs that benefit few should not deny our citizens the best products at the best prices.

I believe that protection breeds inefficiency and non-competitive industries and indeed leads down a slippery slope. I have always believed in the principle of free trade.

One of the great misconceptions permeating discussions of free trade is the illusion that those jobs and those industries that presently exist in our country will remain static and unaltered if we do not enter a free trade agreement with the Americans. So comparisons are made about how many jobs we presently have and how many might be lost. The truth, of course, is quite different. The level of employment and the very existence of industries in Canada are constantly being affected by trade policy decisions made outside our country. They are also affected by multinational agreements to which Canada becomes a party. They are affected by economic conditions elsewhere in the world, and by the pace of development in the third world.

Not so many years ago Nova Scotia had textile plants in Oxford and Bridgetown and elsewhere in the province. We manufactured trucks at Debert. We built deep-sea oil drilling rigs at the Halifax shipyards, and television sets and stereos at Stellarton. The Trenton car works, about which you hear so much, were thriving, with exports flowing to many countries — before those countries, or many of the third world countries, started making rail cars themselves and made the overseas market much more competitive.

All of the jobs associated with the activities I have just enumerated have disappeared as a consequence of international conditions. I do not need to tell you that we have other industries in this province that are presently in jeopardy.

Clinging to the status quo in trade policy is no guarantee of keeping the same types of jobs as we presently have. This is particularly true in our province, where the great bulk of our product goes in export and most of it to the United States. Our fishery, our pulp and paper industry, our gypsum, Michelin tires, Volvo cars, blueberries, Christmas trees, and a vast array of other products head right for the American border.

At the end of World War II we had quite a steel industry in Sydney. It had the logical base for development into a major integrated steel complex, but it did not happen. One major reason was that Dofasco, who owned it at that time, felt it was located too far from the principal Canadian steel markets in central Canada to be competitive. So they left it as an orphan mill and non-integrated, and you all know what has happened to it across the years. Had we had free trade with the United States at that time, with an integrated steel mill at Sydney able to ship into the eastern seaboard of the United States, its future might have been quite different indeed.

While we have lost jobs in some industries, we have been getting new ones as a result of tariff reductions through GATT negotiations. Our standard of living has been higher in recent years than ever before. But whether or not we make a trade deal with the United States, industries will continue to come and go. What a bilateral trade deal does is to provide us with the chance to create new opportunities rather than just be affected, one way or the other, by forces beyond our control.

I have not had the opportunity to see the text of the proposed agreement yet — and I gather that you have not either -- so I cannot give it a blanket endorsement. But I want to applaud the initiative and support the principle of free trade. A fairly balanced free trade agreement would be very much in Canada's interest. We are a trading nation exporting to maintain our standard of living. With 25 million people we cannot possibly consume the things we produce, and therefore we are dependent upon fair winds for trade. It is in our interest to seek the removal of barriers to trade wherever they exist.

When I was minister of trade in Mr. Trudeau's government, I recognized the importance of obtaining better guarantees of access to the vital American market to which we send the lion's share of our exports. I sought to move in that direction by initiating free trade talks with the United States on a sector-by-sector basis. The defeat of the Liberals ended that effort, but I have come to the conclusion that the present free trade project is a more meaningful, more courageous, and an important undertaking — more important than our limited negotiations.

Mind you, the sectoral initiative was an important advance, and all that was possible at that time. What our sector-by-sector approach did was test the waters as to the acceptability of free trade initiatives in the Canadian business community. It demonstrated a broad degree of support for a free trade pact. After the effort was announced, affecting only three or four sectors, we were approached by various other industries asking that their sectors be included. It well may be that the favorable reaction to the sectoral talks affected the thinking of the royal commission that subsequently recommended a comprehensive free trade arrangement.

To date this great Canadian debate on free trade has been characterized by extreme positions, articulated by proponents and adversaries. I have to honestly say to you I find myself at odds with many of the statements made on both sides of the question. I think the important thing is that the question should be treated as an economic, rather than a political issue.

One of the arguments I hear against free trade that I do not think is sound at all is that it might lead to the loss of our sovereignty. I suppose only in 17th century Japan, which forbade all contact with foreigners, could it be said that sovereignty was absolute. When one begins to trade with other countries, one lessens that independence of decision that constitutes sovereignty. On the other hand, you are exercising that very sovereignty by entering such agreements.

It seems to me that in this interdependent global village in which we now live, we still will retain our basic sovereignty regardless of whether free trade comes for all of the world, and that it will certainly not be diminished by the removal of tariffs with the United States. I regard arguments to the effect that Canada will lose its culture and its sovereignty, or its social welfare system as a consequence of this kind of pact, as downright silly.

Some people say that the pressure to compete in the United States under a free trade system will force us to dismantle our social programs. We already have to compete in the United States to sell some $90 billion worth of exports a year. Of our former tariffs with the United States 85 percent have disappeared in recent years. That increasing dependence on the U.S. market has not eroded our social security system. Indeed, during these years the system has been enhanced by expansion of the UI system and by the barring of extra billing for medical services, as well as other improvements. If the removal of 85 percent of the barriers has left our social system intact, why should the dismantling of the remaining 15 percent cause such a change? The answer, of course is that it will not and that such claims are unmitigated nonsense and scare tactics.

The business people who sell that $90 billion worth of exports to the United States have been able to compete without the erosion of our social programs. Why should it be any different with those who would be affected by the removal of the small amount of remaining tariffs and non-tariff barriers?

I would like to say a word about culture. The Maritimes constitutes a pretty good example: 120 years of Ontario dominance in this country has not destroyed the culture of the Maritimes. I do not see how free trade with the Americans is going to affect the Canadian culture. Tell me this, though, how will free trade affect our culture?

> *How will free trade affect our culture? Will there be no more highland dancing in Cape Breton? Will our fiddling championships be taken away? Will the Men of the Deep fall silent? Will they kidnap Rita MacNeil?*

I do not think it will.

We do not need protection in this part of the country for our culture. We find it stands very well on its own feet and that we are able to export it, not only to other parts of the country but to the United States also. Does someone suggest that with free trade we would no longer have highland dancing in Cape Breton, or the highland games in Antigonish? Will our fiddling championships be taken away? Will the Men of The Deep fall silent? Will they kidnap Rita MacNeil? Will the magnificent weaving ability be lost to Cheticamp?

I am afraid that the opposition of many organizations and many people that you will hear from is related to the fact that they do not like the United States. I do not want to make any judgments on that at all. I think I am as Canadian as anyone in the country, and I do not see the question of strengthening our country by having better access to the American market as in any way diminishing my Canadianism.

I believe the greatest assurance of protection of our sovereignty, of our culture, is the maintenance of a strong economy, and free trade with the greatest market on earth gives us an opportunity to strengthen our economy that any other country on earth would give their eye teeth to have.

As I grew up in the small town of Windsor, Nova Scotia, 45 miles from here, I heard my teachers tell me the Maritimes got the short end of the stick in Confederation. Other Maritimers have had the same experience. We have heard it all our lives, I think with good justification. Admittedly since Confederation there have been various efforts to redress the economic inequity of being forced to trade east and west behind tariff walls. We were forced to trade east and west, rather than north and south as our traditional economy had flowed, and so there has been some compensation.

What Confederation meant was that we were at the extreme end of a chain of population islands, 4,000 miles long. It was virtually impossible to locate many types of industries here and have them compete in a central Canadian market, not to mention the more distant west. As an inevitable result our economy floundered after Confederation.

Over the years, a variety of regional development programs have been undertaken by Ottawa as partial recognition of our problem. We have had grant systems that have provided grants only to the growth centres, like Halifax, and then they have tried grant systems that have given them only to the hinterland, for which the growth centres where not eligible. They have tried a great variety of programs and they are still trying them with a new project at the present time.

I think everyone from the Maritimes would have to say none of them has been fully adequate. It does not mean they have not been helpful. It does not mean we have not appreciated them but the problem has not been overcome.

Nova Scotians recognize, mind you, that some tariff policy was necessary in the early formative years of our country, and as good Canadians we more or less willingly accepted the loss of our industrial opportunities. At the same time our consumers subsidized the central Canadian industries, paying higher prices for products manufactured there than we would have had to pay if we could have purchased elsewhere. That continues to this day in the price of automobiles and many other products. In the Maritimes and in the west, we have provided markets for Ontario products all these years. Surely those "infant industries" are now grown to the point that they can leave home and go out on their own, and we parents of central Canada, as the Maritimes have been, do not have to give the amount of support we did in the past.

I believe that Canada has now matured to the point where the highly developed industrial base of southern Ontario, with its sophisticated auxiliary services and magnificent geographic location to distribute into the American market, can not only stand on its own feet, but indeed prosper in a free market. I believe the time has come when the Maritimes should be unshackled from a total east-west flow, and be allowed to benefit from our advantageous position for north-south and international trade.

With free trade, a new day would dawn for industrial and economic development in this province. I have stated my belief that a well-negotiated free trade agreement would be good for Canada on the whole, but I am strongly convinced that it would be better for Nova Scotia than anyone else. Our pivotal position on the North Atlantic sea lanes made companies like Michelin and Volvo conclude that this was an ideal location from which to serve North America.

With barriers removed, we can enter a new era of economic development in this province. A good free trade agreement can be the most effective regional development plan this country could have, and it could move us toward the time when transfer payments will no longer be necessary.

PART THREE:
WILL WE STILL BE
CANADIANS,EH?

Chapter twelve:
we'll still be us — in all
our beauty and warts

Richard G. Lipsey

Mr. Lipsey is senior economic advisor with the C.D. Howe Institute, and professor of economics, Queen's University. From a convocation address at Carlton University, Ottawa, June 12, 1987. Copywright, Richard G. Lipsey.

I am honored by the degree you have bestowed on me today and I am doubly honored by being invited to give the convocation address. What I want to do in my address is to share with you some thoughts about the Canadian identity. But first, let me explain why I have lately been thinking so much about the Canadian identity.

The free trade issue
Back in 1983, I began a study of Canada's prospects as an international trading nation. Rather as I had expected, I found the outlook for Canada troubled by economic events and political decisions in the rest of the world. Rather to my surprise, I found myself driven to the conclusion that the important goals of preserving our existing access to foreign markets, and increasing that access, could best be served by negotiating a bilateral trade-liberalizing deal with the United States.

I published these views, and the arguments supporting them, in a book co-authored with Murray Smith. Since then, I have made literally hundreds of appearances — giving speeches, presenting briefs to parliamentary committees, and participating in seminars and public debates. In all these appearances, I have sought to explain my reasons for believing that a Canadian-U.S. free trade association is the best available route for assuring Canada's future as a trading nation, and for believing that something so simple as a bilaterally-negotiated free trade association is not going to compromise Canada's sovereignty *any more than it is now being compromised by unilateral U.S. action.*

In the course of the debate on the free trade issue, one naturally concentrates on the many important questions that arise from the suggested agreement. There is reason to believe that there will be net economic gains. How large will they be? There are strong pressures operating today to curtail Canadian sovereignty, as well as to force some harmonization of social and economic policies with those in the United States. Will a free trade association strengthen these undesirable pressures, as opponents believe, or ameliorate them, as supporters believe? These are real and important questions.

But when all rational argument is finished, I have found that many Canadians, whether they support or reject the free trade initiative, have a deep-seated fear that the Canadian identity will in some way be lost as a result of such a deal. One can point out that other countries have preserved their national identities as a result of entering into associations that are either similar to or much more comprehensive than the one proposed between Canada and the United States. One can also point out that, although about two-thirds of the barriers to trade between the United States and Canada have been removed over the past few decades, Canadians have not lost their identity, and there is no apparent reason why the effects of removing the last one-third should be any different from past experience. Deep down, however, many Canadians seem to be insecure about their own identity; indeed, it seems to me that this insecurity is monumental, since it leads Canadians to worry that their fragile identity would be destroyed by trading a bit more with the United States. I sometimes wonder if there is not a lot of truth in the old quip that *a Canadian is someone who has a national inferiority complex and is having a love affair with it.*

I am not here to persuade you to accept my views on the free trade debate or to discuss the many important issues of economic gain and political sovereignty that are involved. But I do want to try to persuade you that a distinctive Canadian identity exists, and that it is so deeply rooted in our national experience that trading a bit more with the United States will not destroy it.

The low key Canadian identity

In discussing the Canadian identity, it is helpful to compare it with other national identities. If one often chooses the comparison with the United States, it is only because Canada is closest to the

United States geographically and culturally, so that to establish differences between the Canadian and U.S. identities is to establish the even greater differences between Canada and other, less similar countries. Much of what I say about these comparisons is based on my own experience, but some comes from the writings of others, particularly the American sociologist Seymour Lipsett, who has studied Canadian-U.S. differences in great detail.

There **is** a strong Canadian identity, and one of its most distinctive characteristics is that it is very low-key. If Americans wear their patriotism on their shirt-sleeves, Canadians wear theirs sewn inside their undergarments. The concept of being 100 percent Canadian seems as unnatural to us as the concept of being 100 percent American seems natural south of the border. Could you imagine a parliamentary committee on un-Canadian activities similar to the House un-American Activities Committee made famous by the late Senator Joseph McCarthy?

The Canadian identity is so low-key, in fact, that we are often not aware of it. For my part, I never thought much about it until, many years ago, I became a visiting professor at the University of California at Berkeley and sent our children to local schools. Around Christmas, my wife and I found ourselves saying, "You know, we are raising foreigners." Nothing anti-American, or pro-American, was implied, just the simple observation that the attitudes we could see developing in our kids were profoundly foreign to us.

I rather like the low-key nature of the Canadian identity; I rather like the fact that we do not wear our patriotism on our shirt-sleeves. Our cool approach to being Canadian, however, creates problems when we are called on to judge issues such as supporting Canadian cultural industries or negotiating a free trade association with the United States. We only obscure the real and important problems involved in such issues when we think that the very basis of our national identity is at risk.

What, then, is the nature of this low-key identity? First, I will say a bit about what it is not.

What we have in common with others

The Canadian identity does not make us utterly different from every other people in the world. Today, many cultural and behavioral patterns are found everywhere. Technological developments in communications guarantee that. They have made the world smaller and have created some substantial homogenizing pressures on our economy and on our day-to-day life. One can buy McDonald's hamburgers and Kentucky fried chicken not only in New York and Toronto but in London, Paris, Tokyo, and Bangkok. One can get Coca-Cola even in Moscow and Beijing. British programs dominate drama on U.S. public television, while U.S. sit-coms and detective dramas are popular throughout the English-speaking world, and beyond. Movies serve an international market; those made in the United States, through sheer numbers, dominate the English-speaking world, but Australian and British movies, and some recent Canadian successes, are also seen around the world. So cultural isolation is no longer possible even if a society wants it. We may deplore, or laud, these developments according to our individual values, but the homogonizing forces exist and apply universally, not just to Canada. But just as the Danes are no less Danish for sharing in this universal culture, so Canadians are no less Canadian.

Canadians also share many common experiences with all North Americans in general and with citizens of the United States in particular. These create some basic similarities among us, while setting us apart from people in other continents. We live in a vast new continent, where what we find old seems laughably new to people in Europe and Asia. The immigrant status of all but the tiny minority of original occupants is still fresh in our collective memory. Few North Americans can go back beyond their grandparents without finding at least one immigrant, and many have a much more immediate experience with immigration.

But just as the Scots stay Scottish and the Irish stay Irish in spite of having many experiences and characteristics in common with the English, and just as the French stay French and the Germans stay German in spite of sharing some common heritage and experiences with other Europeans, so we Canadians stay Canadian in spite of having a set of experiences and characteristics in common with all other North Americans, and an even larger set in common with residents of the United States.

Canadian groups

These are some of the things we share with others. What, then, makes us distinctive? Speaking in generalizations — as I must in the brief time at my disposal today — I distinguish five main groups of Canadians:

• the indigenous people, who were here before the European invasion;

• the original French colonists;

• the original settlers from the British Isles, together with later immigrants from the same stock;

• older immigrants, who came before the Second World War; and

• newer immigrants, who were part of the waves of people who, starting in the 1950s, came first from Europe and then from all over the world, and who transformed, and are still transforming, Canadian society. (It is hard to believe that the "Toronto the good" I knew as a graduate student from 1951 to 1953 has become the cosmopolitan wonder that is, in my opinion, one of the five great English-speaking cities in the world today.)

Historical experience

Going back to our early history, we find a dramatic difference between Canadians and Americans. On the one hand, U.S. society was based on a revolutionary experience, a violent breakaway from the authority of the British crown. In Canada, on the other hand, Francophones and Anglophones, who were the dominant groups until after the Second World War, both had a counter-revolutionary heritage.

Francophone society was based on a rejection of the ideals of the French Revolution. Whereas post revolutionary France became a secular, increasingly urban society, French Canada remained a church-dominated, predominantly rural society. Francophone society has changed rapidly in the postwar decades, but the cultural heritage of this background remains.

The small original Anglophone population was given a decisive increase, and an important attitudinal slant, with the influx of refugees from the American Revolution. These United Empire Loyalists fled the United States because they rejected the ideals of the Revolution and wished to remain loyal to the British crown. They were true counter-revolutionaries, who gave a distinctive character to Anglophone society, particularly in Upper Canada.

Unlike the United States, Canada had no war of independence. Instead, our independence evolved over two centuries. This highly-civilized process is something in which Canadians can take pride, but it does not provide the same dramatic movie material as does the American Revolution. Here is one of the many reasons why our identity is low-key, while the U.S. identity is much more "up front."

Heroes and myths

Canadians have no strong military tradition. During the War of 1812, Americans twice invaded Canada and were repelled. But most of the fighting on our side was done by British troops. Many Canadians fought willingly in two world wars, but our peace-time military has never had a strong presence in the public mind. Unlike the United States and many European countries, we have never fought a bloody civil war. No general has ever been prime minister of Canada, in dramatic contrast to the United States, where there is a tradition, stretching from George Washington to Ike Eisenhower, of electing successful generals as presidents.

Another related part of our low-key, nonmilitaristic character is that we are not given to hero worship. "Trudeaumania" came as close to it as we have ever been with respect to our political leaders, but such emotions are as rare in Canada as they are common in the United States. A more typical Canadian attitude is that displayed toward William Lyon Mackenzie King. A distinguished leader who, in his time, was the longest-serving prime minister in the British Commonwealth, Mackenzie King was greeted with universal titters whenever he appeared in newsreels (*the* media for animated visual news for my pre-TV generation). Compare this embarrassed detatchment of Canadians from their leader with the universal hatred or love (depending on whom you asked) that Americans felt for Mackenzie King's contemporary, Franklin D. Roosevelt. Even at the age of 12, it struck me forcibly that there was something very different in the way in which Canadians and Americans regarded their respective national leaders.

Canadians are not great myth-makers or myth-believers. We neither generate great outpourings of pro-Canadian propaganda nor believe much of the propaganda that we do generate. Anyone who has had serious dealings with Americans, no matter how much respect they have for them, has noted the difficulties inherent in relationships with people who believe deeply in their own national mythology. Let me give you one of the many available examples.

Americans tend to see international politics as a battle between the forces of good, currently led by the United States, and the forces of evil, currently led by the Soviet Union. Among other things, this leads Americans to support even the most horrible tyrannies as long as they profess to be anticommunist, and to oppose relatively moderate regimes that indulge in the rhetoric of the left. As one senior Canadian diplomat recently said to me, "Canadians don't like dictatorships, Americans don't like dictatorships of the left."

Geography

Strong geographical forces also shape the Canadian identity. All North Americans tend to see themselves in a battle of man versus nature (and only lately have some come to worry about not destroying important aspects of nature in the process). Among North Americans, however, Canadians tend to see themselves as a small band of people up against a vast wilderness — the second-largest country in the world inhabited by a mere 25 million people. Americans, on the other hand, tend to see themselves as victors over nature — 250 million people in a slightly smaller and certainly more benign part of the continent.

The effects of this different view of nature can be seen in many ways, including the novels we read and the fictional heroes with whom we identify. Canadians often identify with the heroic failure, someone who fights a glorious battle against the forces of nature, or fate, but who ultimately loses. Americans are more inclined to identify with the triumphant victor over seemingly overwhelming forces, even when it stretches credulity to believe that anything but defeat could have come out of the situation. Looking at nature, "survival" is the name of the game for Canadians; for Americans, it is "conquest."

Government as a partner

Our evolutionary background and our geography have helped to create among Canadians the view of government as a friend, an inevitable partner in our attempts as individuals to tame a hostile environment. To Americans, more of whom came from continental Europe and whose history includes the experience of throwing off British rule, government is a potential enemy. Since their part of the continent was conquered more by individual than by co-operative effort, Americans see no reason why government should be a necessary partner in their exercise of individualism.

Canadians have much greater respect for law than is typical of Americans. I have stood on a street corner in Toronto with a single other pedestrian, and with not a car in sight, waiting for the light to turn green — behavior unimaginable in most large U.S. cities (or, I should add, in Montreal or Quebec City). Attitude surveys of Canadians show a much higher respect for, and trust in the honesty of, the police than found among Americans. Canadians commit far fewer murders. Canadian cities work, are clean, and are relatively safe in ways that few large U.S. cities are. In what country but Canada could a *police force* — the RCMP — be a much-loved national symbol?

Our view of government as a partner has given Canadians a solidly based, small-l, liberal tradition. Americans, under presidents from Roosevelt to Johnson, had their liberal period, but then they joined much of the rest of the world in a "shift to the right." Under Ronald Reagan, many of the New Deal and Great Society programs have been dismantled, and poverty has increased substantially. Canada has also had its "shift to the right," but the Mulroney government's modest measures look positively socialistic when compared to those of the Reagan administration. Indeed, such is the strong Canadian attachment to our whole set of social programs that a conservative government has been reluctant to touch them even where, by common consensus among experts, they need substantial overhaul. Can you imagine Ronald Reagan speaking of his "sacred trust" to preserve the existing social welfare system root and branch?

The point of my argument is that there are deeply ingrained differences between Canadians and Americans, not that one of us is better than the other. To make that point, let me give you a major example of where I prefer American attitudes.

Respect for personal liberty

One of the things that follows from some of the characteristics I have already mentioned is that Americans have a much stronger sense than do Canadians of the importance of personal liberties. Americans start with the attitude that the state is the enemy and that "eternal vigilance is the price of liberty." One way in which this attitude is manifested is in the American belief that the ends do not justify the means if the means include any infringement of the personal liberties of Americans. (I wish I could say the same for their attitudes toward the personal liberties of Central Americans). For example, evidence that the police gain through illegal means is forever tainted and cannot be used in U.S. courts. No doubt, some guilty persons avoid prosecution as a result, but Americans see this as the price of protecting their liberty. In their view, allowing tainted evidence to be used provides the police with a strong incentive to infringe on personal liberties — by making illegal searches, for example — in order to gain evidence that they suspect exists but have no legal means of obtaining.

Canadians take a different view. Most of us are more inclined to believe that if the ends are important enough, such as bringing a dangerous criminal to justice, the means can be justified even when they include infringement of personal liberties. As a result, in Canada, evidence obtained in searches that are not strictly legal can often be used in subsequent legal proceedings. There is no doubt that individual liberties have sometimes been infringed on as a result, but Canadians seem to feel that the state can be trusted to exercise a measure of restraint and only indulge in such behavior when the ends really do justify the means.

I do not find myself agreeing with this attitude; my reading of world history tells me that individual liberties are very fragile and that the state all too often does become the enemy of personal liberty. So, in this crucial aspect, I wish Canadians were more like Americans. Be that as it may, every thoughtful observer who has looked at this aspect of social attitudes has had no doubt that there are profound differences between the characteristics of the two peoples.

The immigrant experience

Another way in which we are different is in our immigrant experience. In the United States, society was transformed by the enormous waves of immigration that occurred in the late nineteenth and early twentieth centuries and that largely ended by the 1920s. Although Canadians had an important influx of immigrants during that period, and although these immigrants transformed the societies of many regions, the influences of the established Anglophone and Francophone communities remained predominant throughout that period.

In Canada, the immigration that transformed the national society began after the Second World War and has yet to end. The racial mix of the immigrants was different in the two countries, with a higher proportion of non-Europeans coming to Canada. Attitudes also differed among European immigrants to Canada, many of whom were not fleeing political persecution or genuine famine to anything like the same extent as were the earlier immigrants to the United States. Of course, we have opened our doors to refugees from Eastern Europe and Asia, but partly by virtue of the times in which we live, and partly because of the different economic and political conditions in Western Europe, attitudes of the typical immigrant to Canada in 1960 differed from those of the typical immigrant to the United States in 1880.

I could go on listing national difference for literally hours, but already I am running short of time. I have, however, saved what I regard as the most spectacular illustration of our unique national identity to the last.

The separatist crisis

When the United States passed through its crisis of national unity, the issue was settled by a bloody civil war. To say this is not to cast aspersions on Americans; their behavior was par for the course — throughout history, most people have resorted to arms when presented with the possibility of a breakup of their nation.

A decade ago, Canada had its crisis of national unity. With the election of a PQ government in Quebec, the breakup of the country became a distinct possibility. And what did Canadians do? Did we follow the example set by most of the rest of the world and rush to take up arms against each other? No. We took to the debating stand, we held seminars, and in countless other ways we talked, and we talked, and we talked. While we argued, bureaucrats in Ottawa worried, not about battle plans, but about the vexing problem of how such national capital as the armed forces would be split up in the event of Quebec's separation!

And when the national debate was over, what did we do? We had a vote. And who voted? The province considering secession voted; the rest of us watched while making it clear that if Quebecers voted for separation, then separate they could. Go to Sri Lanka, East Timor, Spain, France, Iraq, China, or India, to mention just a few countries where separatist minorities are currently being subjected to military or police persuasion and see what response you get if you were to suggest that the secession issue should be settled by a vote taken solely in the area where the minority communities reside.

We resolved our conflict over national unity in a way that has few precedents in all of recorded history — I can think of less than half a dozen. As movie material, our experience palls beside the United States' dramatic and bloody civil war; can you imagine a Canadian David O. Selznick producing the epic "Gone with the Referendum?" But as a civilized method of conflict resolution, it stands superior to almost all other historical experiences. If that is not something to be proud of, I do not know what is. Yet, such is our low-key Canadian identity, such is our reluctance to blow our own horn, or even to know we have a horn to blow, that most Canadians regard the resolution of the 1970s "Quebec crisis" as something to be embarrassed about and quickly forgotten, rather than to be proud of and remembered as setting a standard of civilized behavior for all time.

Conclusion

So there it is. There **is** a distinct Canadian identity. It is deeply rooted in our history, our geography, and our human experience. Like all other national identities, it has warts as well as beauty spots. In many cases, the latter are very admirable indeed, and the former — like them or not — help to make us what we are. It is an identity of which we can be justly proud. Long may it stay low-key. Long may we not be national chauvinists. Long may it last and, although it must evolve in ways that are hard to foresee under the impact of heavy immigration, we can be confident it will stay distinctive.

So when you come to make up your minds on the Great Free Trade Debate, listen to all of the arguments and try to assess the evidence. Some of you will then decide you are for and some of you will decide you are against the proposal. That is your privilege as a citizen of a democracy. But base your decision on how you appraise the real economic and political issues that are at stake, not on the mistaken belief that the Canadian identity, of which we are justifiably proud, is so skin-deep that it will not survive eating one more McDonald's hamburger, watching one more installment of Dallas, or doing five percent more trade with the Americans. Do your country, and your national identity, the honor it deserves by understanding that it is more than skin-deep; that not only is it admirable, it is also deeply rooted, and that whatever sensible or misguided policies we follow in the future, our identity as Canadians will be around for quite some time.

Chapter thirteen:
an artist views free trade,
culture and equal opportunity

Christopher Pratt

Mr. Pratt is one of Canada's most outstanding artists. He lives in St Mary's Bay, Newfoundland. From a presentation to the House of Commons standing committee on externals affairs and international trade, St. John's, Newfoundland, December 4, 1987.

I apologize for not having a typewritten, duplicated submission, I do not have access to those services where I live in Newfoundland. Indeed, everything I know about the recent history of this debate comes to me through the CBC, which is the only television station I can get, thanks to some vagaries of the CRTC, I believe.

I have the privilege of appearing here as a private and individual Canadian and Newfoundlander. I am by trade and profession a painter and a printmaker, but I am not today representing any group or lobby or faction, nor do I presume to present any views other than my own.

I understand the depth and sincerity of the anxieties expressed by many people in the arts community regarding the concept of free trade with the United States of America. I respect their integrity. I share their commitment to Canada, but I do not share their anxiety. Because of the increasingly partisan and politicized nature of the free trade debate across Canada, which I consider to be entirely regretable — indeed, the stridently partisan tone of most public discussion in Canada is an aspect of our culture that I could do without right now — I feel it is not inappropriate for me to tell you that I am not a member of any political party, nor do I habitually support any one political party on the basis of doctrine or dogma.

My sense of solidarity is with the people who seek a better way of doing things, who try to do what they do well. I believe that toeing a party line does not serve this present process well. It may be that much of what you are hearing is compromised by being partisan, that submissions may not always accurately describe the best interests of the constituents they purport to represent. It is apparent that many aspects of the free trade proposals lend themselves to emotional interpretation, wherein appeals to patriotism are tempting and easily made on both sides. It is very easy to assume and then to act out a role on either side of this debate, and the issues are far too important to be loaded aboard an existing, ongoing political bandwagon.

I would also like to express more than a little sympathy with those members of your committee who are frustrated at having to conduct these hearings in such a short timeframe, and in the absence of what would appear to be an elusive final draft. On the other hand, perhaps you will understand my anxieties about this process, when I read in the press that minds are made up and minority reports are anticipated — even before your group leaves the capital city.

I am in favor of free trade. There are many well-reasoned, well-documented, deeply felt and intelligently held positions on both sides of this proposal, but I believe the arguments in support of free trade with the United States are more compelling than those against it. I believe in the fundamental logic of continental trade as a vehicle whereby Canada can achieve a more equitable economic balance and opportunities coast to coast, which so far have eluded us and are very long overdue.

In the first decades of this century an overwhelming social concern was the fairer distribution of wealth. Great strides have been made in this area, which have provided a measure of dignity and security to millions of Canadians who would otherwise have little of either. That process is not yet complete. However, it seems to me that there is now another, more urgent issue, which has as much to do with human dignity as the redistribution of wealth, and that is the more equitable distribution of work and the more equitable distribution of economic opportunity.

Once upon a time it was a matter of taking from the rich and giving to the poor, and many wealthy and privileged people, who constituted a reactionary establishment, opposed it mightily. They sought to keep what they had. They did not want to share. They opposed change. They liked the status quo. No one would brand as a reactionary someone who does not want to lose meaningful work. No one would equate the right to a meaningful and productive job with the luxury of wealth. It is not a matter of wanting to snatch a job from one person or one area and give it to another. But in an overall economic strategy, and to achieve a fairer distribution of work opportunity, we will have to lose jobs in some sectors where perhaps we cannot be competitive, by virtue of climate or geography or whatever, in favor of more jobs and more secure and naturally viable work opportunities in sectors where we are and can be competitive. We may in fact have to do without the ginger ale of champagnes. We also have to be prepared to see more of those work opportunities distributed fairly and equitably across this nation and not remain forever concentrated in a few small areas. We have to guard against reaction to such change and recognize reaction for what it is, wherever it shows up.

If you live in a community and you work in an industry where you have work all the time, then things are all right for you and things look pretty good the way they are, and change is an alarming prospect. You are apt to forget that when the automobile was put into production it put out of work most blacksmiths, harness shops, that it ruined the market for hay, and ended forever what now seems to

> *We do not need a nationalistic, chauvinistic posturing in our arts. The strength of Canadian culture is precisely that it is part of an exciting, vital, open North American culture.*

have been a lovely way of life — silence, the clip-clop-clip of hoof on road, and sleigh bells in the snow. But few would return to those days now, except perhaps in the temporary nostalgia of this time of year — certainly not the citizens of Oshawa or Oakville.

You are apt to believe that make-work projects, the provisional proverbial 10 weeks, achieves this fair distribution of work. Make no mistake, much of Newfoundland, many communities, many thousands of people could not survive except in desperate poverty without these programs. At best they are acknowledged band-aids, but they are certainly not the necessary surgery. They more closely resemble an anaesthetic, and the patient is waking up, uncured, realizing that what we need is a more fundamental redistribution of work and economic opportunity in Canada than these schemes have ever provided or ever will. People are beginning to realize that the surgery is needed at the centre, not the extremities.

A lot has been said about the potential of free trade to destroy Canadian culture and Canadian indentity. Perhaps it is because I have been a Canadian for only 38 years that I have never been able to discover precisely what Canadian culture is, although I have listened attentively to debates. I have participated in them. I served for six years as a member of the Canada Council. I know it is a mistake to try to define Canadian culture by drawing a line along the 49th parallel.

North America is not a continent separated into hard distinct little countries that are the residue of centuries of wars and bitterness. It is not a continent of fiefdoms and kingdoms. It is not a continent of walled cities and iron curtains and Berlin walls: nor should we erect them now. We do not need a nationalistic, chauvinistic posturing in our arts. The strength of Canadian culture is precisely that it is part of an exciting, vital, open North American culture. It is not a monolith. It is not an assembly of protectorates. There are networks of cross-fertilization that go east and west, north and south, and proceed diagonally across the continent, happily ignoring the 49th parallel.

Nonetheless, Newfoundland is not Ontario. New Brunswick is not New Hampshire. But neither is New Hampshire, New York: or Houston, Harlem. In North America, it seems to me, cultural separateness is rich even where it is subtle. It relates to geography and history and climate and the strength of individuals in communities in that environment. It does not need to be forced. Indeed, it is at its most ludicrous when we attempt to force an identity by changing the size, for example, of a football, by going to three downs instead of four, by pretending that the shows we put on in Canada are not direct apes of shows in the United States, such as the Oscar shows, by pretending that Canadian artists do not aspire to showing in the United States, do not want to have their movies distributed in the United States, and all that kind of thing. Those are the aspirations of most Canadian artists, Canadian culture. Canadian identity does not need the stuffy incestuous enclosure of a greenhouse environment to survive.

In 1949, at least until April Fool's Day of that year, we had in Newfoundland and Labrador a British government, an American army, Canadian currency, our own postage stamps, and three Departments of Education. We should have been having an identity crisis. We were not. We knew who we were. We did have a crisis of confidence, especially confidence in our ability to govern ourselves. We had the option of trying to do that and seeking an economic association with the United States, or joining Canada. The latter option you may be amused to remember was billed as British union by those who wished to fan the fears of the stars and stripes. I believe we joined Canada not out of fear of Uncle Sam but out of a deep and probably well-justified fear of our own politicians. There were those who feared that either way we would lose our Newfoundland identity, and there are many who think we have.

Clearly, though, we have not. On the contrary, even with full political union with Canada, the culture and unique identity of this "now province" has flourished. Many, many Newfoundlanders, artists and otherwise, have done exceptionally well, given access to that broader audience, that greater and more secure prosperity. Many artists and teachers have worked and prospered here. They have enriched our own outlooks, our abilities, and our performance.

If the Newfoundland identity could survive total economic and political integration with another country, why do Canadians see the removal of some remaining barriers to trade with the United States — a nation whose culture we already borrow from, learn from, and contribute to, and with no thought of political or institutional union — as a threat to our identity?

In my own discipline we work without direct protection from the foreign product. Paintings and other works of art enter this country duty free. When you and your colleagues next go into an art dealer, or wherever you go to buy a work of art, which I am sure you all do frequently, your decision on what to procure will be based on what you like, what you think is good, and what speaks to you as Canadians, not on some small artificial prop.

There is nothing in this draft agreement that will prevent or discourage Canadians from buying Canadian prints or paintings, reading Canadian books, watching Canadian dance or movies or television, or attending Canadian theatre if they want to. Indeed, as long as committees such as this continue to roam Canada there will always be Canadian theatre.

Indeed, greater prosperity and more work security will increase access to and expand the availability of these things to all people. I believe the ability of the fiscal offices and the cultural agency to stimulate and facilitate production in the cultural sectors is fairly protected in the draft agreement.

Many people have expressed anxieties over the potential difference between the spirit of an agreement and its eventual application. Nobody knows more about that than Newfoundlanders. When we entered this Confederation in 1949, we thought that, when the British North America Act talked about freedom of trade across provincial borders, that was what it meant.

I agree with the Premier of this province and thousands of other Newfoundlanders — in fact, Canadians everywhere — that one of the greatest injustices in this nation is our own inability to get our electricity to market through or across the province of Quebec. As you have heard, oil flows uninterrupted east: electricity stops dead in its tracks at the Quebec border.

Is oil a commodity and electricity a concept? We know a contract is a contract is a contract. We know the historical circumstances of the Churchill Falls contract and all the truisms about hindsight. We also know that, if the shoe had been on the other foot, had Quebec owned the resource and had this fledgling and impoverished province stood between it and a market, we would have had a delivery system rammed through us from vent to voice without apology. For nearly 40 years we have been forced to deal with a sister — or is it a brother? — province, and through it Canada, as if it were a foreign country.

We know about the national interest clause. Can it be in the national interest to keep one province forever at the bottom of the heap? We are at the bottom of the ladder, with nothing above us but missing rungs. Is it in the national interest to placate the strong at the expense of the weak? That is what we fear. That is not the way we want the free trade issue to be resolved.

We see missionaries fan out from the prosperous core across this land to defend the status quo, but the status quo is not good enough.

Finally, may I say a word about the lobster. It has a claw that crushes and a claw that carves, but either way it has to escape its shell, and without one be temporarily vulnerable growing a bigger shell. That may very well be what we have to do. If it is , then I believe we should begin the process.

Chapter fourteen:
where's the beef?

Mordecai Richler

Novelist, journalist and scriptwriter, Mr. Richler is a two-time winner of the Governor General's award. From a presentation to the House of Commons standing committee on external affairs and trade, Ottawa, November 18, 1987.

Parliamentary debate since the deed was done has not helped to clarify the issue. It has been characterized by more partisan push and shove than illuminations. I do believe Mr. Broadbent is stating his case from conviction, but I suspect that Mr. Mulroney and Mr. Turner could switch chairs and argue each other's briefs with just as much simulated-for-TV outrage and sincerity. After all, they are merely lawyers. What they appear to be clashing about with such deep feeling is the keys to the office next time out, not the future of this country, an iffy nation from the beginning, the economic interests of its regions often bitterly at odds.

I want to put on record my impatience with the more extreme positions being taken on both sides. The nationalists have made some telling points. They are addressing questions about our cultural survival that should concern all of us, but I do object to the most strident of them appropriating the grandiose title of Council of Canadians, as if those of us who have not yet made up our minds or who are honestly for the deal are anti-Canadian or non-Canadian.

There is also a rich irony that I cannot resist. For as long as I can remember, the nationalists have complained about the indignity of our branch-plant economy, and now — hello, hello — many of them are raging because if this free trade deal is cut they say there will be no more need for branch plants here. Those damn Yankees will shut them down and go home. This, however, does not make them nationalist Nazis, as Mr. Reisman so ineptly put it.

On the other side of the fence, I am also appalled to find indecently rich Ontario protesting so much. Westerners, Maritimers, and many of us in Quebec's distinct society have been forking out for Ontario's over-protected goods for years, when it would have been cheaper and more convenient to shop over the border. I hate to be caught agreeing with Ronald Reagan about anything, but if free trade meant the dubious wines of Niagara would be displaced by the far more palatable stuff distilled in California, I would not be displeased.

There is only so much plonk I am prepared to drink for my country. In fact, the louder I hear Ontario squeal, the stronger my support for free trade.

Let me take this a step further. If I were trying to market this deal for the Tories, I would run full-page ads in newspapers throughout the other nine provinces, saying "You Can Help Screw Ontario-Support Free Trade."

Many of my colleagues feel the free trade deal as presently constituted threatens our cultural survival. That would be insupportable, if they were right. I understand and agree with their case as related to film policy, but I do not quite grasp the threat, if any, to book or magazine publishing. Let me deal with book publishing first. I am speaking of English-language book publishing.

In principle, I am for more Canadian ownership of our book-publishing firms. Hell, I am for more Canadian ownership of everything here. But there are problems. First, publishing everywhere is going increasingly international. Recently my British publisher was acquired by Americans, and a firm I deal with in New York is now German-owned. Just as Conrad Black has acquired the Daily Telegraph, there is no reason, say, Avie Bennett could not take over or start a book-publishing firm of his own in London or New York. Furthermore, it is ridiculous to regard Americans or British who publish books here as interchangeable with Attila the Hun.

It should also be noted that Canadian ownership of itself is no guarantee of quality. There are some admirable Canadian-owned firms here — McLelland & Stewart, Lester & Orpen, and MacMillan — but there are others who are just shlock merchants, packagers of non-books. I find it instructive that Mel Hurtig, Captain Canada himself, has never, to my knowledge published a new Canadian novelist or poet. In fact, foreign-owned cultural imperialists such as Penguin Books or Doubleday bring out more first novels by Canadians in a season than Hurtig has since his firm was conceived.

I have read that Canadian book publishers put out 85 percent of books written by Canadians but account for only 20 percent of the revenues of books sold in this country. I do not find these figures as alarming as others do. Indeed, I think them heartening, a tribute to the talent of Canadian writers. But after all, we are cultured people, and we also want to read the best that is being written in the other Americas, North and South, in Europe, Asia and Africa, and these books come to us largely through foreign-owned distributors. Once the population of this country has doubled, it will be possible for Canadian-owned firms to bid for these rights, claiming Canada as a separate market. In fact, it has already begun to happen.

Meanwhile, I should tell you that writers are not badly off here. For young writers, there is the Canada Council, a splendid organization I would like to see blessed with more funds. All of us have reason to be grateful to the present government for finally enacting the public lending library rights bill.

Alice Munro, Margaret Atwood, Mavis Gallant, Robertson Davies and myself, among others, sell far more copies of our books in this country on a per capita basis than do writers of comparable talent in the United States or England. Furthermore, we were not drafted to do our jobs. We volunteered. We are not owed an audience or applause or grants simply because we were born here.

> ## There is only so much plonk I am prepared to drink for my country.

If the free trade deal is a threat to indigenous book publishing or novelists, I fail to get the point. I do see one possible threat, but I have no idea if it is on the table. As things stand, Canadian-owned firms receive block grants from the Canada Council for publishing so many works by Canadians. What if the Americans protest that this constitutes an unfair trade advantage? What then? Publishing new young writers in this thinly populated country is a quixotic venture, and these grants will be absolutely essential until we are, say, 40 million here. I would want to think again if these grants became chips in the trade deal or are vulnerable to future pressures.

I have read that our magazines feel menaced because under the terms of the trade deal they will have to pay the same postal rates as imported publications, but I suspect they are overstating the case. Let us look at a couple of our most popular general magazines. Maclean's and Chatelaine. I do not consider either one a cultural artifact, any more than I do Time, Newsweek or Cosmopolitan. I also take it that Maclean-Hunter, a huge conglomerate, is highly profitable. Indeed, I remember reading somewhere that in the last decade their stock value has soared. Why cannot they lick the same number of stamps as Time or Good Housekeeping?

Saturday Night, easily our most intelligent general magazine, is a different case. It has always lost money, as far as I know, and I doubt that a marginal increase in its mailing rate will prove terminal. Furthermore, it should also be noted that if Saturday Night has always lost money then it is certainly not because it is suffering from a uniquely Canadian disease. That virus is universal. Magazines of similar quality in the United States and England, say the Atlantic Monthly, Harpers or The Spectator, are also unprofitable. Just as Conrad Black will now be carrying the bucket for Saturday Night, so will other rich entrepreneurs bolster Atlantic Monthly or The Spectator. They write it off as a tax loss against more profitable ventures. Looked at in another way, in the end it is the poor guy on the assembly line, somebody who would probably much rather read Hustler, who is paying the bill, just as anybody who is taxed at source shoulders an unfair share of most of our bills.

If free trade really does mean a net gain of 350,000 jobs — and I am far from satisfied by the evidence offered so far — then I do not think anybody but a zealot would quibble over the postage bill of Maclean's.

Flora MacDonald's proposed film legislation struck me as highly intelligent, as a bill that would have done much to encourage our film-makers; but I take it that it has been abandoned in response to pressure from Ronnie. If that is the case, it is too damn bad. I hold no brief for our film producers. Most of them are con men, creative only in their mastery of double bookkeeping and tax jiggery-pokery. Unlike their Australian peers, they have not signed the cultural skies with their honor, but have instead darkened them with their insatiable greed. If certain tax loopholes are to be closed, then certainly they brought it on themselves by taking outrageous advantage of them. If private investment has dried up, it is because private investors have been cheated twice too often.

But there are a few honorable producers here. There are some gifted directors, performers, writers, and especially technicians — film-makers of genuine talent who deserve the country's help and protection. Given a chance, they might map the territory. They will make films of real Canadian content that can be enjoyed anywhere. I would hate to see them abandoned.

Finally, I have to come back to my original point. What has been agreed to? What benefits will accrue? I am willing, even eager, to be convinced; but I need more evidence. Meanwhile, like Margaret Atwood, I do not trust futurologists, those wonderful fellows who study the entrails, and gave us Mirabel Airport, marginally more convenient to Montreal than it is to Labrador City. I want to see more hard facts, less partisan conjecture. We are being rushed into this, a kind of shotgun wedding, in order to cope with Congress's so-called fast-track timetable. But this is still a sovereign nation, more or less. What about our timetable, our need to hear more?

I say hold a referendum, call an election. I do not know. Let the people hear and absorb both sides of the argument, and then we shall decide.

Chapter fifteen:
Canada's culture cadets
and our national identity

Earle Gray

From an address to the Federation of Women's Institutes, Argyle, Ontario, October 1, 1987.

Those who advocate a free trade deal say it will result in more jobs and more money. And even those who oppose a deal, usually don't dispute this claim. Their argument is really based not so much on what free trade would do for Canadians, but what it would supposedly do to Canada. We are expected to believe that by helping Canadians, free trade would somehow hurt Canada. We are told that it would be the beginning of the end for Canada. At worst, we would become swallowed up by the United States. At best, we would become merely a mirror of America. No longer — we are told — would we be entirely free to make our own decisions about such things as health care programs, government subsidies of all types, farm marketing boards, unemployment insurance, social programs, protection and help for our cultural industries, and all the other things that politicians want to have the power to decide for us. And everything that makes us distinctive, that makes us Canadian — our art and culture, books, newspapers, magazines, films, music, radio and television broadcasts — will be swamped by the great American tide if we sign a free trade deal. Our national identity will be washed away in the American ocean. That, at least, is what we are told by a great number of our artists, writers, broadcasters, publishers — the people whom I think of as Canada's culture cadets.

I happen to think that the culture cadets are dead wrong. I am convinced that the biggest threat to a viable, desirable, positive Canadian identity would be *failure* to achieve a free trade agreement. My fear is that without the benefits of freer trade, our cultural activities — from the Winnipeg ballet to Woodville minor hockey — will simply become less affordable. And those activities that do survive will become more dependent on taxpayer generosity and the unpredictable decisions of politicians and bureaucrats. As one of the smallest publishers in Canada, that makes me very apprehensive.

No one knows more about the benefits of trade, from firsthand experience, than farm families. If it weren't for trade, farm families would, for example, make all their own clothes. You would probably raise your own sheep, make your own wool, and sew and knit all your clothes. You would tan the hides from your cattle and make your own shoes.

Farm families are very resourceful, and I know that you're entirely capable of making your own shirts and shoes. But I don't know of any who do. The reason is simply that it doesn't pay you to spend all the time that would be needed. You spend your time to produce those things you have found it pays you to produce — milk, eggs, beef, pork, corn, wheat, whatever. And you buy those things that it doesn't pay you to produce or make. You are much better off when you sell what you produce best and buy what others produce best.

This simple, elementary truth prevails, whether we're talking about farm families or nations. For example, we could grow right here in Canada all the bananas we could ever eat. It would require some humungous green houses, we'd have to burn horrendous amounts of fuel, and we'd need import restrictions so that we couldn't buy much cheaper bananas from the Banana Republic. Canadian consumers would lose because it might cost you as much as $1.98 to buy a banana for breakfast, and Canadian producers would lose because the Banana Republic would stop buying our wheat, and timber and telephones.

But if we ever did erect a tariff that allowed us to grow our own bananas, it would be very difficult to get rid of. The Banana Growers Association of Canada would say, "Look, we've invested billions of dollars to build banana green houses, and if you allow those cheap imports, all that investment will be wiped out." And the Amalgamated Canadian Banana Pickers Union will holler, "Hey, there are 400,000 Canadian jobs at stake here."

There is no mystery about what will happen if our trade with the United States becomes more restricted. We will have fewer jobs and less income. It's as simple as that.

No one but a few economic Neanderthals any longer dispute the fact that, although some difficult adjustments will be needed, freer trade will give us more jobs and more money.

But it has not yet dawned on the culture cadets that there is a connection between what we earn and what we can afford to spend on our culture. Our culture cadets worry that the billions of dollars of taxpayer money now spent to subsidize Canadian culture might be endangered under the terms of a free trade agreement. They are blind to the fact that these subsidies are already endangered, *because we can't afford them.* And if we suffer economically by lack of a free trade agreement, we'll have to cut back our culture spending even more severely.

That might seem a little remote right now. We've had six years of sustained economic growth, and here in Ontario there is virtually no unemployment. But these threats will be far more real when the tough times come. And you know that the tough times will come. Tough times are just around the corner. They always are. Economic recession follows economic growth as surely as night follows day. What we don't know is when the next recession will come, how long it will last, and how severe it will be — whether it will be simply another recession, or another depression. What we do know is that if we have trade restrictions, the tough times will come sooner, hit harder, and last longer. And we'll have a lot less money — whether it's tax money or the spending money of individual Canadians — to spend on our culture cadets.

I'm sure that the state will always perform a larger cultural role in Canada than it does in the United States. To me, one of the most distinguishing traits of our national identity is that we always seem to walk down the middle of the road. We don't entirely trust free enterprise, and we certainly don't trust socialism. Compromise is another name for Canadian. Nothing in excess. So our cultural industries will continue to be a mixture of private initiative, state enterprise, and public subsidy. Institutions like the CBC, the Canada Council, the Canadian Radio-Television and Telecommunications Commission, and the National Film Board will continue to play an essential role in sustaining Canadian culture and expressing our national identity.

Like most Canadians, I endorse the need for such institutions. But like most Canadians, I also worry about anything carried to excess. And I'm worried that the extent to which our cultural industries rely on government support has become, indeed, excessive. It makes our cultural industries very vulnerable, for two reasons. It makes us vulnerable to any cutbacks in government spending. And that concern will be increased if we lose the economic advantages of a free trade agreement with the United States. And secondly, it makes us vulnerable to government control — which might be an even greater worry.

If taxpayers continue to spend billions of dollars a year to subsidize our culture, to what extent will our cultural industries become increasingly controlled by politicians and bureaucrats? A former president of Imperial Oil once warned other oil men that if they ran to the government for a Band Aid, they would come out in a straight jacket. To what extent will our cultural industries find themselves in a government straight jacket? Do our newspaper, magazine and book publishers, our broadcasters, film producers, actors, and musicians, feel completely free to criticize government spending, while at the same time receiving, every year, billions of dollars in government support?

One way or another, public support seems to pervade almost

every aspect of publishing, broadcasting, and the arts. Let me touch on just a few examples.

A few weeks ago I got a letter from Pierre Berton. Perhaps you did too. Mr. Berton wrote to a lot of people on behalf of Friends of Public Broadcasting seeking support to oppose "the slow demise of public broadcasting in Canada" and "massive cuts to the CBC." Then in the mail last week, I received a copy of CBC's latest annual report. It says that for the year ended last March 31, the CBC spent $1.1 billion — $45 million more than the year before. That doesn't seem to me like massive cuts. Some $800 million of what the CBC spent was charged to taxpayers. That's an average of approximately $100 for every household in Canada. Canadians cherish the CBC and I suspect that most of us are willing to pay to keep it going. But I also suspect that, if we were ever asked, most of us would say that $100 per household is ample — maybe even too much. Of course, no one knocks on your door to ask, "How much would you like to donate to the the CBC this year?" But you pay it, just the same.

Last week I also stopped in the library to look at the last annual report of the Canada Council. The Council spends close to $100 million a year "to foster and promote the study and enjoyment of, and the production of works in, the arts." A lot of this money goes to writers and publishers. Just for fun, I jotted down the list of the various types of grants issued to writers and publishers. It includes — now hold your breath — block grants to publishers, project grants to publishers, translation grants, international translation grants, travel assistance for translators, aids to periodicals for promotion campaigns, periodical contributors' remuneration fund, aid to promotion and distribution of Canadian books and periodicals, grants for promotion tours for Canadian books and periodicals, book publishers promotion fund, literary prize book kits, national book festival, public readings by Canadian writers in residence, public readings by Canadian writers in the United States, public readings organized by Canadian writers' associations, short-term writers in residence programs, writers-in-resident program, Canada-Scotland writers-in-residence exchange, the National Association of Writers and Publishers, and finally, grants for national conferences. Is there anything that writers and publishers do without the help of government? Hundreds of publishers and publications benefit from these grants, from Canada's largest book publisher, McClelland and Stewart, to Ragweed Press, Dandeloin Magazine, Germination Review, and what sounds like an exciting book called The Politics of Reproduction.

One title that you will never find on the list of Canada Council grants is Canadian Speeches. My wife and I funded this publication with our own money. Well, actually with money that I borrowed from the Royal Bank. But at least the debt is entirely ours, and we are going to either sink or swim without the help of a government lifejacket. I want to feel completely free to publish speeches by the president of the CBC (as we have) as well as by those who think that the CBC ought to cast off without a penny.

I must confess, though, that I may, in the past, have benefitted from a few Canada Council grants, although I'm not absolutely certain. After publication of several of my books, I have gone on promotional tours across the country, arranged and paid for by the publisher. This is where authors are interviewed on radio and television by people who have never read their books. Although my publisher never told me — and I never asked — I suspect that the costs of the very few such promotional tours that I've made as an author have been covered by Canada Council grants. As soon as I can afford the time and money, I intend to write several more books — without any government grants to either write or promote them.

The CBC and the Canada Council are only two of the many sources of public support for Canadian culture. Provincial government spends their share. About eight years ago, as the result of an application by my publisher, I received in the mail from the Ontario Arts Council, a completely unexpected cheque for about $1,500. It was the first I had ever heard of the Ontario Arts Council. Unfortunately, none of the money wound up in my pocket. My publisher for this particular book suggested I spend the money on a promotional tour. Perhaps he hadn't succeeded in getting a Canada Council grant. I don't know.

But there are still more ways to spend the taxpayers' money. Authorized second class mail privileges for periodicals, such as Canadian Speeches, is one. I think that magazines and newspapers are, in fact, entitled to less than first-class mail rates, because they are mailed in volume and because they are pre-sorted and bundled, which significantly reduces the cost for the post office. But the rate is set so low that second class mail is carried for practically nothing. As a publisher, I don't want to have to pay excessively expensive first-class mail rates, but at the same time it's hard to justify the dirt-cheap rates of second-class mail. I'm confident that our subscribers would pay a reasonable charge to have Canadian Speeches delivered to them.

Finally there are the tax breaks enjoyed by film and television producers, and publishers — and these have to total very large amounts of money. Most books, magazines and newspapers are exempt from provincial sales taxes as well as the federal sales tax. When you buy a package of writing paper in Ontario, you'll pay seven percent provincial sales tax. But not when you buy the Toronto Star, the Sun, or the Globe and Mail. The break on federal and provincial taxes saves publishers about 20 percent on newsprint costs. And it's a break that many publishers really don't need. There may be many book publishers and publishers of small periodicals that struggle along with little or no profit. But overall, the publishing industry is the most profitable industry in Canada, each year earning an average 25 percent return on invested equity. I certainly don't begrudge publishers whatever profit they can earn in a competitive market — and I want to earn as much as I can — but again it's difficult to justify taxpayer support to help generate those earnings.

You know that the federal government intends to overhaul the federal sales tax — probably after the next election. The general idea is to apply a lower rate of tax, but with fewer exemptions. I think that's a good idea. However, you can bet there will be a long parade of privileged people — including publishers — seeking to maintain their exemptions. But here is at least one publisher who intends to stand up and say that publishers and their subscribers should pay the federal sales tax, along with everybody else.

Canadian Speeches is a very small drop in the ocean of Canadian culture. But I believe that our small publication has an important contribution to make to the expression of Canada's national identity. Our task is to make widely available, for the first time, a previously unpublished treasure of Canadian thought and literature — the speeches by leaders from every field of endeavor: politicians, business people, academics, labor leaders, scientists, people who range from Governor General Jeanne Sauve to Canada's Nobel prize winner John C. Polanyi.

But I can assure you that establishing a small publication like Canadian Speeches on a national basis, is a real challenge. It is a precarious venture.

I also happen to believe that, in the long run, our best chance of success lies in the support of our subscribers, rather than the support of the taxpayers. And I also know that if we are to succeed, Canadians must earn enough that they can afford such things as Canadian Speeches. And that's why I favor the freest possible trade with the United States and, indeed, with the whole world.

PART FOUR:
INTERNATIONAL POLITICS
OF PROTECTION AND
TRADE

Chapter sixteen:
The politics of
protectionism in the U.S.

Allan E. Gotlieb

*Mr. Gotlieb is Ambassador of Canada to the United States. From an
address to the Institute of Corporate Directors, Toronto, January 28,
1988.*

Crying "wolf" is a dangerous business. Crying "sheep" when in
fact there is a wolf at the door is more dangerous still.

There are those in Canada who say that protectionism in the
United States has gone away, that the wolf is a lamb after all. Opponents of the Canada-United States free trade agreement, in particular, are seizing on this alleged metamorphosis to argue that we
face no threat and need no agreement.

The argument goes something like this. Pressure for omnibus
trade legislation in the United States was greatest from 1986 to the
fall of 1987. Since Black Monday, jittery financial markets have sent
signals that passage of such legislation would hurt rather than help
economic growth. Moreover, the most recent (unadjusted) monthly
trade figures show a 20 percent decline in the U.S. deficit, and rising
U.S. exports. And finally, Congress is leery of risking action that
could leave it bearing at least part of the blame for a possible
recession.

In fact, the wolf is still a wolf and is still at the door. Protectionism
is still alive and well in the United States. It is not a short-term
phenomenon. And the Omnibus Trade Bill is not its only manifesta-

tion. Indeed, this type of legislation has not been its principal manifestation in the past and may not be again in the future.

Today I want to talk about the politics of protectionism in the U.S. I choose the U.S. because it is by far our largest market. But please understand that I am not saying for a moment that protectionism is not a problem in the other major countries, including our own. Of course it is and it is a serious and growing one. But implications for Canada of protectionism in the United States are unique.

For a number of reasons, in the United States the politics of protectionism have overtaken the policy of trade promotion since 1979, when trade liberalization reached its zenith with the conclusion and implementation of the Tokyo Round.

First, American economic and technological leadership has been challenged. A revitalized post war Europe, a disciplined and dynamic Japan, and the recent emergence of the newly industrialized countries, particularly on the Pacific Rim, have shifted comparative advantage and dynamic efficiencies away from the United States to these other areas of the world. Major industrial sectors, such as steel, automobiles, textiles and machine tools, have suffered major declines in the United States. Global market conditions have forced a contraction in U.S. agricultural production.

Perhaps it might be said that the stock market decline of "Black Monday", on October 19, was at least in part a response to the failure of business to undertake the adjustment necessary to face up to the challenge of growing international competition. And now the United States still finds itself with a number of declining industries that require massive re-investment to face increasing international competition.

As American self-confidence was shaken, the very vocabulary of trade began to be altered. Only a few years ago the key words were "free", "open" and "liberal" trade. Now the current lexicon demands "reciprocity" and "fair trade" on "a level playing field". Now even "competitiveness" is often used as a code-word for protectionism. In today's cultivated language, the wolf of protectionism is trying to dress itself in the innocuous cover of sheep's clothing.

These economic developments are reflected in the political arena. In earlier decades, the Democrats, the farmers, the unions and the consumers formed the basic free-trade coalition. Many — perhaps most — Democrats have changed their stance, as have the unions and, increasingly, the farmers. The old coalition has shattered. The Democrats remain, generally speaking, the majority legislative party and, of course, they now control both Houses of Congress. And the Democrats' electoral base — the northeast, the south, the minorities, and labor — is likely to continue pushing the party in the direction of protectionism.

There are signs that the United States is beginning to face this challenge of declining and uncompetitive industries. There is a growing recognition that severe problems of education, of competitiveness, of attitude and of management must be addressed. But the cure lies in the long-term, and meanwhile there is, alas, a pronounced tendency among some politicians and public figures — not the administration, I hasten to add — to view the principal problem as one of unfairness on the part of America's trading partners.

Certainly there are unfair trading practices in the world. The United States is right to complain about these practices, as we are in Canada. We are all guilty to some extent, and must seek to eliminate trade distortions.

But unfair trading practices are not, in the opinion of most, the principal cause of the worsening U.S. trade balance. Rather, U.S. trade has deteriorated as a result of macro-economic forces that have challenged U.S. superiority in traditional areas of industrial strength. The administration and many leaders in business and Congress are trying to face up to the long-term challenge. But the overwhelming pressure remains to seek short-term solutions that are responsive to particular or special interests at a micro-economic level.

The U.S. political system has undergone rapid change in the past two decades and is now under increasing strain. In the Congress, the seniority system has ended. Power is dispersed and diffused. There are no more political bosses who can readily control or deflect damaging initiatives. The legislative agenda is now largely run by a greatly increased number of committee and subcommittee chairmen, who, in this arena, are perhaps the most powerful players in the United States system. They interact with special interests seeking narrow legislative fixes. The end result is often "gridlock" in the system, or, alternatively, open season for the special interests.

Fragmented power in the executive branch itself provides another convenient avenue for special interests to seek narrow fixes. The White House must often arbitrate among powerful competing interests represented by various departments in situations too innumerable to mention.

Declining industries are also able to harass foreign competition through litigation before autonomous agencies, such as the International Trade Commission. Decisions by regulatory bodies often affect trade adversely, even in the guise of purely domestic regulation, as, for instance, in the "as-billed" rule promulgated by the Federal Energy Regulatory Commission (FERC).

Increasingly, even the courts are affecting the regulation of international trade through their interpretation of U.S. law in specific cases. Domestic tribunals have little institutional competence in the field of trade and are given virtually no opportunity to consider and weigh broader U.S. interests or foreign economic policy interests. Thus, in litigation between the Environmental Protection Agency and a U.S. uranium producer, a Denver court last year sought to enforce a complete embargo against all imports of this mineral.

Political scientists tell us that the policy-making process in Western pluralistic democracies must mediate among competing

> **Beset by worries and growing protectionism, the U.S. is nonetheless the most democractic, pluralistic, accessible, open, and vigorous society on earth.**

interests rather than between political parties. And indeed, any representative government must be responsive to domestic interests. Based on my experience, however, it is my belief that the U.S. system, because of the highly-fragmented nature of power, makes it increasingly difficult for the interests of other countries or the international system itself to be brought effectively into play at critical times.

These various factors combined make quite a potent recipe and the protectionist pot continues to bubble merrily away. Let me give you a few examples.

•U.S. pork producers, losers in a countervail case against Canadian imports, went to Congress and succeeded in obtaining an amendment to the omnibus bill that would, if passed effectively reverse the decision.

•U.S. lumber interests, dissatisfied with the result in the softwood lumber case of 1983, managed to have a second case accepted and actively lobbied Congress and the Administration in the course of obtaining a negotiated settlement with Canada in 1986.

•The threat of a "safeguard" or "escape clause" action has induced Japanese automakers to accept voluntary restraints since 1982, even though these restraints are of questionable validity under the United States' own antitrust laws.

Despite the long-term phenomena I have described, some observers still insist that U.S. protectionism has reached its peak and is now receding from view. Support for the omnibus trade bill, they say, is waning and it is now far less likely to be adopted. So let us all heave a sigh of relief and go back to sleep.

I don't want to make predictions about the future of the omnibus trade bill. It may or may not pass. At this moment no-one can say for sure. But the kind of argument I have just described confuses the medium with the message. The omnibus bill is exactly that — a medium or a method. It can be seen as an omnibus -- or a train if you like-carrying many special interest passengers. It may run out of fuel -- but again it may not. In any event, it is only one of many vehicles available on the protectionist road.

In fact, over the last few years, U.S. protectionism has expressed itself through various "ad-hoc" measures rather than through any redefinition of trade law. Here are a few examples of typical devices.

Quotas: Steel trade with the United States is now administered through quotas, or voluntary restraints, which resulted from a safeguard action and threatened legislation.

Buy America: Exports of Canadian cement have long been threatened or limited by such provisions of U.S. law.

Special rules: Canadian participation in U.S. government procurement is limited by small business and minority set-asides, and by special rules on defence production imposed in the name of national security.

Today, even if the U.S. trade deficit declines significantly — and there is some question about how quickly that will happen — protectionist pressures will continue. Remember that the U.S. economy has expanded impressively over the last five years. Remember also that U.S. unemployment is the lowest in the west except for Japan. But there continue to be important industrial "losers" in the United States. The number of "losers" will no doubt increase when the expected recession comes. And the system permits them to carry on and on to seek more protection, regardless of the general state of the economy. Here are some recent examples of specific Congressional legislative initiatives in the energy field alone:

•Senator Domenici has sponsored legislation to restrict imports of uranium from Canada.

•Senator Bingaman introduced the "Imported Natural Gas Fair Treatment Act" in December 1987, to put barriers in the way of Canadian gas imports by adding to the regulatory burden for such imports.

•In the House, representative Rahall introduced the "Environmental Equity Act" in October 1987, to restrict Canadian electricity exports by imposing new environmental regulations on Canadian power production destined for the United States."

In the last session of Congress, over 14 "Buy America" riders governing procurement were attached to the budget continuing resolution.

Outside Congress, other protectionist forces continue to work without benefit of new legislation.

An anti-dumping action against potash from Canada and other countries raised the cost of fertilizer to the American farmer by 60 percent, although a negotiated settlement recently reduced the margin of duties.

•Another anti-dumping action has recently been launched against imports of structural steel.

•A group of U.S. oil producers last month launched a "National Security" investigation on oil imports.

•U.S. customs has tightened regulations governing the labelling of goods containing imported products.

•An oil import fee is being actively debated by the presidential candidates.

•Trade in steel, automobiles, textiles and a range of agricultural commodities such as sugar and dairy products is now administered, quite independently of market forces, under a range of quotas, orderly marketing arrangements, and voluntary restraint arrangements.

I think the evidence is more than sufficient to demonstrate that protectionism is a long-term trend. It has been with us for some time and is likely to continue for the foreseeable future, whatever the fate of the omnibus trade legislation this year. Economists have estimated that whereas approximately five percent of U.S. trade was administered in the mid-1970s, over 30 percent will be governed by some sort of restrictive regulation by 1990.

Please don't get me wrong. All is not gloom and doom in the United States. We should not let America's economic difficulties obscure our appreciation of its enormous economic importance and its impressive overall economic performance. We should not let the difficulties of the U.S. system blind us to its vitality and strength. The United States remains the most democratic, pluralistic, accessible, open and vigorous society on earth.

There are still free traders in the United States. Plenty of them. President Reagan is one of them. And there are many in the Congress too.

But protectionism is my theme. And protectionism remains a long-term problem for those whose trade depends on access to the U.S. market. Successive Canadian governments have recognized this. In 1983, the Liberal government of the day undertook a sectoral free trade initiative, proposing liberalized trade in specific areas such as steel, telecommunications, agriculture, and subway cars. They discovered that sectoral negotiations, limited to narrow areas, would not permit the trade-offs nor the overall benefits to Canada that would flow from more comprehensive arrangements.

Prime Minister Mulroney, for his part, ordered a renewed study of the issues involved and solicited the views of Canadians across the country. After considering the options, the government proposed comprehensive free trade negotiations to the United States in October 1985. Discussions began in earnest in May 1986, and concluded with the signing of the free trade agreement on January 2 of this year.

So, as you can see, the free trade agreement is not a product of panic, nor a simple response to the omnibus trade bill, nor to allegedly short-term protectionist forces in the U.S. wrongly perceived as about to expire. It is intended to address deep and persistent protectionist forces at work in the United States. To counter the influence of declining industries in the U.S. system, it encourages long-term solutions rather than short-term fixes, and seeks to substitute the rule of law for the politics of trade.

The free trade agreement is much more than a defensive system in any event. It is no panacea but it provides a framework for the management of the closest and most complex trading relationship in the world. It sets out principles to bring the North American economy into the 21st century.

There are no miracle cures for economic ailment. But the agreement represents a historic turning point. It brings together within a larger market two economies with different resource endowments and productive capacities. It thus permits increased specialization and economies of scale, supporting the comparative advantage of each. Politically, it sends a signal to our trading partners that trade liberalization is both possible and desirable, and points the way to agreement in the GATT in the fields of service and investment.

If reason prevails, the free trade agreement will be approved and implemented in both countries. It stands on its own merits as a "win-win" proposition that is good for the United States as well as for Canada. And it is crucial to the success of the Uruguay round of multilateral trade negotiations.

More important still, the agreement is crucial to Canadian, U.S., and global economic health. As the **Washington Post** reported last Sunday, analysts are no longer asking whether a recession is in the offing, but rather when it will arrive. Black Monday has taught us that continued growth cannot be forever consumer-led. Prosperity for the United States, as well as for Canada, must come from growing international trade. In 1987, U.S. exports rose by 20 percent. They already account for over half the current U.S. growth rate. The free trade agreement will enhance the rate of growth for both Canada and the United States in each country's largest export market.

So there are two replies to be made to those who say protectionism is a spent force and that accordingly we do not need a free trade agreement. First, protectionism is with us still. Second, the free trade agreement goes well beyond the issue of protectionism to address the issue of growth.

Chapter seventeen:

has American money ruined Oshawa?

Grant Devine

Mr. Devine is Premier of Saskatchewan. From an address to the Empire Club of Canada, Toronto, December 3, 1987. Edited for publication.

This morning I had a fascinating tour of the GM facilities in Oshawa, and while I was going to come down here and save Ontario from the United States, I decided to join you. Not only the rest of the country would envy what I saw today, but indeed the rest of the world. It is absolutely phenomenal what is taking place in southern Ontario, because of the technology, because of the efficiency, because of the economies of scale, because of the information that is being used, the training, everything I saw. I'm absolutely convinced. If I had some doubts about it before I got here, I don't have any doubts about it now. What has gone on between the U.S. and Canada, in Ontario, has been phenomenal.

I got into politics because I thought the country was perhaps going in the wrong direction. In my part of the world, in the seventies, I found the governments nationalizing industries and closing up the borders, and buying out investment, and all my economic and business training told me that either everything they taught us in university was haywire, or there was something wrong with the country, and certainly something wrong with some of the leaders who were taking us in that direction.

I've had a fundamental belief in more trade and more freedom internationally — fundamental from my own economic thought to my personal feeling about how we developed in Saskatchewan. All four of my grandparents were immigrants. They came to this country to build, and they did. And there were thousands, and tens of thousands of people just like them. So I am a fourth-generation Saskatchewan individual who wants to build, and I get extremely frustrated when I find people who get in the way. Love them but I either want to go around them or over them or through them or something, because I want to continue to build.

So today I am here because it's been a long mission for me to see if we can open the doors of opportunity for our children — my children and yours. Open them, not close them. And open them not only locally and nationally, but indeed, internationally.

October the 19th was Black Monday, and the market fell a great deal. It was very similar to 1929, and it reminded me of things I had learned about that era, and I'm sure it might have reminded people in this room a little bit of some of the things that took place 50 years ago.

In 1929 we had the stock market crash. Governments made two fatal mistakes in 1930. The United States passed the Smoot-Hawley Act that doubled tariffs, and they raised interest rates. They did both because they thought they could protect themselves from any disaster, and it was exactly the wrong thing to do. Other countries retaliated. We doubled tariffs and others doubled tariffs, and by 1933 there was massive unemployment across Ontario, across Saskatchewan, across United States and across the free world. High interest rates and the high tariffs were exactly the wrong thing to do and we suffered for a long time. We certainly did in the west.

Well, after that we got even more serious about tariffs — we went into the Second World War. We got serious enough to say, "we're not only going to stop trading with you, we're going to make sure you can't trade at all." What do you do in war? You apply sanctions, you blow up their bridges, you cut off their communications systems, and you blow up their ports and their railroads. Why? Because you want to hurt them, you want to slow them up. Well, we applied all that and more, and we were successful. We won the war, but the world lost. We lost all the productivity and all that wealth, and those families that were destroyed. But we certainly learned how to hurt countries. We learned in 1929 and 1930 and we learned in the war.

Since the Second World War we've started to do things a little differently. All the smart countries got together with the General Agreement on Tariff and Trade, to reduce tariffs. By the 60's about 60 percent of the goods and services traded between the U.S. and Canada were tariff-free. Today, it is about 83 percent, and the remaining tariff averages about 10 percent.

I go through that little bit of history, because here we are again. We've had a stock market crash. And people are saying, "Well, I wonder what we should do?" Should we have this big omnibus trade bill in the United States that doubles tariffs? Should we raise interest rates? Clearly, history has shown that when you want to slow somebody up, you apply tariffs. You apply sanctions. For heaven's sake we're even talking about applying sanctions to countries in Africa, and it isn't to help them, right? It is to hurt them. Now just say it again, so that nobody has any misconceptions. If sanctions hurt, and more sanctions hurt more, then less sanctions must help. You can't have it both ways.

Now here we are today. We've been reducing tariffs and reducing tariffs between the Japanese, Americans, Canadians, Europeans and others, and we have been doing pretty well. How well? About $150 billion a year in two-way trade between the U.S. and Canada and about $90 billion between the U.S. and Ontario. Ontario does more trade with the United States than any country in the world, most times. Japan and Ontario sort of compete for first place. I think Ontario now does more business with the United States on a percentage basis than the State of California does with the United States. It's been quite profitable, because we have lowered tariffs between the two countries.

Our economy has been hurting, because internationally, people have been playing unfairly. The price of wheat has gone from $7 a bushel to $2.50. How would you like your wages or salary cut by two-thirds or three-quarters? That is exactly what has happened. The farmer is just as productive. Europeans and Americans have decided to take their treasuries and just unload money as incentives. The United States spends one billion dollars a year just in storage of surplus grain.

If you have a subsidy and I have a subsidy, and if people have more and more subsidies, they get antagonistic, and they don't want to trade with each other. So they put restrictions on my potash, and restrictions on my meat, and restrictions on the uranium, and on the oil, and on the pulp and paper, and on the steel. One thing leads to another and pretty soon you're in a conflicting situation where nobody's making any money and you're calling on the taxpayer to bail everybody out. We're into deficiency payments now here in Canada, taking on the U.S. Treasury. We have the same sort of conditions that led up to the big problems in 1929, 1930, and 1935, that led to conflict generally.

I can't find a reason why I would want to go out and raise tariffs against somebody else, and increase subsidies as a solution. It's always seemed to me to be a problem.

Let's keep the tariffs going down. Let's have some sort of a mechanism that we all get in the same room and talk to each other, eyeball to eyeball, rather than telling stories about each other, on each side of the border. Some sort of a binding mechanism. Let's harmonize our laws the best we can, because we're each other's best neighbor, and the largest trading partners in the world. It seems to me that's all we've got left.

That's what we're facing today — an opportunity. An opportunity to change the direction, not only of that country, but indeed the destiny of this country — and in my view, the destiny of the free trading world and probably the entire world, with one example. A very historic example.

People will say this is not perfect, this deal that we're going to cut with the United States. And they're right, it's not perfect. The question is, is it better than where we are today? Or where we have been? And is it in the right direction? I would argue that it is, and I'll give several reasons for that, again in a few minutes.

The biggest argument I get when I travel across the country is that we would be too close to the United States if we lowered our tariff some more. We'd be too intimately tied to the United States. We would really be in some trouble. So I came here to Ontario to see the best example that I know.

What's the best example of being closely tied to the United

> *We will have to face all the problems of adjusting – adjusting to lower prices, more jobs, better jobs, greater opportunities, more money.*

States? Right here in this room. You. How are you? Are you okay? You bet you're okay. You're fine, thanks. Probably among the best off in the world.

And that's why I went to Oshawa, because I heard that there were Americans going crazy in Oshawa spending all this money — billions of dollars of American money.

It was getting so serious that I was worried about your culture, worried about your sovereignty, worried you'd lose your religion, you wouldn't watch CBC, you wouldn't even listen to CBC, because the Americans were investing all this money in your back yard. How awful.

So I went to see how bad it was. And I was there. I went to the mountain, and I've returned. And it was beautiful. It was great. GM alone is investing 8.1 billion dollars, 1980 to 1990 in this nice little triangle here. Forty-five thousand employees. $1.6 billion a year in salaries-every year! Do you know how much money that is a month? New homes, new cars, new mortgages, investment and prosperity and wealth and schools and roads and hospitals and all the things you can build with productive people.

Prosperity. I saw it in spades this morning. Absolutely in spades. Not just the envy of the other parts of Ontario, or the country, but indeed the world. The diversification, the specialization, the productivity based on knowledge. Talk about knowledge-based industries, economic development, high-tech, the training and retraining that's going on in Oshawa alone -- it is phenomenal. Productivity is up from 45 trucks an hour to 60. Same people, better trained. All those things. Quality jobs, better jobs, and better and better and better opportunities.

Some would say, "You know, if we had all this investment and we're close to the United States, we'd have to adjust." What an adjustment, right? We'd love it. Adjust to those new jobs, that kind of training opportunity, that kind of competitiveness, that kind of pride in the new tech, and the high-tech, and the information-based world.

I asked them at GM this morning, "Why Canada?" They said because of the productivity, and frankly, because of the wage structure which is extremely competitive, and the social structure, which is extremely competitive, and the exchange rate. That's why they're here. Eighty percent of their product goes into the United States.

What I found out this morning is that I'm not here to save you. I'm here to join you. I'm here, as a Canadian that says I'm proud of Ontario. I'm proud of your ingenuity. I'm proud of your courage to do that. And when I think about my children, I want to see the same courage for the 21st century. I don't want us going the other way. I want to go forward, as their grandparents did, and as you did, and as they want to do.

People ask me if we will lose our sovereignty if we trade too much. The Europeans in the Economic Community have a common market. They're not worried about their sovereignty. Greece just joined. They figure it'll take five million years to change Greek culture, now that they're in the Economic Community. They're not worried about their culture. Come on. Only if you're strong enough to go into the community of the world, will you build and maintain your culture, not by hiding. That's the cowards.

Someone says it's too much investment. Would I ever like the problems of too much money! If we got it piled up so much, and just had money, and money in investment, well, we'd maybe have to tax some of it back, or we'd have to regulate some of it and redistribute it, because we'd have so much. And we'd have built too many hospitals, and too many services, and too many good highways, we'd just have too much money.

I spend half my time as a premier searching around the world, soliciting people and countries and investment to come to Canada. And people are saying, when the opportunity's here, that we should turn it down?

So if it isn't sovereignty, and if it isn't our culture, and if it isn't too much money, is it adjustment? Well, if we lowered tariffs we'd have to adjust. I hear about the adjustment, for example, that would take place in the textile industry that lives behind tariffs in central Canada. And I ask, why would we ever want to confine those people, particularly women, to just that job? Why would we want to confine them to that when they could have better jobs? Higher paying jobs. More jobs.

There's more adjustment going to take place in the exchange rate from day to day than you'll see in the tariff. There's more adjustment in the interest rates from day to day than there will be in the tariff. Try adjusting to two-dollar wheat. Or when oil drops from $35 a barrel to $10 a barrel. Interest rates from 10 percent to 20 percent. Try that on for size in adjustment.

Some have said we're not big enough to do this with United States. Seems to me that Ontario's big enough to do it alone. You're bigger in trade with the United States than any other country. You're bigger than many states trading with the United States. You have shown the way. You are way out ahead of everybody else in the world, with the biggest trading partner there is. So Canada can't do it? You've got be kidding.

Then again, some have come back and said, "Well, we can't do it." And I hear this all the time from the premiers that are not really in favor of it. They say, "I believe in free trade." Right? They say that. Believe in free trade, and freer trade with the United States but this deal isn't quite good enough. Not quite good enough. Let me just say that if you cut a deal with the United States, and all you did was agree to have tariffs go to zero over 10 years, I'd take it. Forget the rest of it, we'll live the way we are right now but we agree that tariffs will go to zero in 10 years. I'd agree to that. It's going the right way.

What have we done in addition to that? We said we would have a binding dispute settlement mechanism. It's not perfect, but it's a lot better than the one that is there today. And we've agreed over seven years to harmonize our laws to make them better, more consistent. Is that bad? No. That's what they told us to do immediately. Couldn't get it done immediately, but you can do it over time.

Then there's the argument, that we don't have guaranteed access to the U.S. market. That's what they told us. "Guaranteed access to the U.S. market is not perfect, therefore I'm not taking it." Let me say, and I said it yesterday at the agricultural ministers conference in Ottawa: How do you expect to have guaranteed access to the United States market, when you go into the deal telling them that you want to cheat? You want regional development policies, which means regional subsidies. You want supply management, which says you won't trade in those goods. You want beer carved out, because you don't think you can handle it. You want various kinds of things protected to start with, when you go to the table. To those in the Maritimes who say, "I don't have guaranteed access," I say if you want to give up regional subsidies, they'll probably give you access to the U.S. market entirely. "Well, I can't do that." Well, then you won't get it. They're not stupid. They're sitting across the table and saying, "You don't want to trade these things? You want a little bit of cheating going on, you want to subsidize this, you don't want to trade that, you want to be able to do this and so forth? Yeah, okay, well then we'll saw it off someplace less than perfect."

What do you expect? Do you expect to have supply management, and all the marketing boards you want, and all the culture and all the things you'd like to have, and have the United States just open its doors and you can still cheat a little bit? No. You can't. Because they're going to say, "We want to cheat a little bit, too." So, that's where you saw it off. They have supply management, all kinds of commodities. They said, "You leave our milk alone, we'll leave yours alone." Fine, we won't touch each other. You can saw it off. But don't let anybody tell you that we're going to get guaranteed access to everything in the United States and we can play by a different set of rules.

Some have said, "But they still have countervail and antidumping." If you design a perfect trade deal in theory, what does it say? "We agree to live by these rules, and you won't cheat, and if you do, you're going to get called on." That's countervail. You're going along trading in whatever it is -- widgets, coats -- and somebody decides to fork up a bunch of tax money into that industry which is going to export to the United States. They're going to call you on it. That's countervail. So you get a binding dispute settlement mechanism where both countries can sit down and look at it and judge it and find out if you really are playing by the rules. And that's exactly what's been done.

Then they'll say, "They probably won't do it because the protectionist side of the argument is easier." Now that one has some smack. That's the one I'm most fearful of.

It is awfully easy to sell the protectionist side. You go to the people in Oshawa who are working, and say to them, "If you have a free trade deal, you'll lose your job." You can knock on doors in Saskatchewan, and you can be with our largest private employer, Intercontinental Packers — makes bacon, sells it into 25 or 30 states — they love Canadian bacon. Great. You knock on the doors of those folks, and you say, "I'm here to protect you from the United States," and they'd say, "good!" If anybody's going to protect them, they feel good. If you went to them and said, "I'm going to lower tariffs and give guaranteed access to the United States in a free trade deal," they'd kind of look at you. "What's this, free trade? I don't understand that." The protectionist side is easy, and it has been for centuries. It's dangerous, but it's so tempting and so easy.

So when I look at free trade, it's not perfect, but it's perfect in principle. This deal is not perfect, but it's perfect in principle. Lower tariffs, it's good for us, it's good for Ontario, it's good for Saskatchewan, it's good for the country, and indeed it's good for the world. There is no economic argument that says we shouldn't pursue this. I've looked at all the economic arguments — from adjustment to higher tariffs to lower tariffs to productivity to new jobs and better jobs. I'm challenging all premiers, and I'm here today to challenge the premier of Ontario to join me in building a better Canada, building a better Saskatchewan, building a better country, and indeed provide an example for the rest of the world, in that kind of building. You have in the past, why quit on it now?

Now finally, my friends, I want to say that the world needs an example. If two of the finest, most sophisticated, mature nations can't cut a deal, who else is going to do it? We need one good example, internationally. We need to show the Japanese, we need to show the Europeans in particular, we need to show the Chinese and the Soviet Union. We need to show the whole world how to put together a relationship between two mature countries and say, "This is the way we'll do it." I need it, I tell you. In the General Agreement on Tariff and Trade, I need to have agriculture fixed and then have the countries back out of subsidies and back away from protectionism. The number one irritant, world-wide.

It's good for peace, the more you're interrelated, connected with Japanese and Americans, and all other people. Hundred of millions that need our food, need our help, need access to Canadian markets, and we need access to theirs so that we can increase their prosperity, and they can make a living and not just be dependent on aid.

I find no economic reasons for higher tariffs. Political reasons to no end, but not economic. But I believe this opportunity we have here as Canadians, this time right now, is very historic, not only for Ontario and Saskatchewan and indeed this country, but for the world, and I hope and pray that we have the courage to take up the challenge.

Chapter eighteen:
It's time to stop the
agricultural warfare

Lorne Hehn

*Mr. Hehn is president of United Grain Growers Limited. From a
submission to the House of Commons standing committee on external affairs and international trade, Winnipeg, November 27, 1987*

For 81 years United Grain Growers has worked to further the
economic well-being of farmers by providing commercial services
and considered views on farm policy issues.

There is no doubt that western Canadian farmers are facing a
marketing challenge as tough as any they have faced in the century-
old history of the industry. Those in touch with agriculture are
abundantly aware of the nature of the problem. Canada is being
caught in a growing tide of protectionism world-wide and in the
crossfire of a trade war. As in any war, the notion of fair play and
proper conduct are forgotten. Innocent parties are being hurt.

The fallout from this war is having severe impacts on prairie
agriculture. In fact, it is shaking the economic base of western
Canada's economy. Aggressive acts by others in the world market
have led to sound defensive measures by the federal government,
and it is clear that until hostilities cease defenses must be maintained.

But in spite of the fact that world agriculture is in a truly sorry
state, it is also a time of opportunity, we suggest. A GATT round has
started and the elements of the Canada-U.S. trade agreement have
now been signed.

In thinking about the past and the opportunities to come, we must
keep in mind that the problems we see today come from a widespread
unwillingness to be flexible. It would be far easier for United Grain
Growers to come before this committee and cite a list of demands and
amendments to the Canada-U.S. free trade agreement — but that
approach applied around the world has led to where we are now in
agriculture, and if continued it will lead us nowhere.

The realities of today's grain markets are far removed from the
basic theories about trade that are the building blocks of negotiation.
In today's agricultural markets we must simply get back to the
basics. And, we submit, the lessons from agriculture should be
thought about long and hard by those who feel the basic concepts are
nothing more than airy-fairy academic principles.

Let us walk through some of what has been happening in recent grain markets, to underscore where lack of free trade can lead. This September the Saudi Arabians, who make up 40 percent of the world market for barley, changed their import policy. Before the change they were granting importers a subsidy of $80 U.S. per tonne to import a product worth about $65 U.S. per tonne.

For those who do not have a feel for what $65 U.S. means laid down in Saudi Arabia, it translates into about $40 per tonne Canadian for barley at Thunder Bay. And taking into account rail freight subsidies and handling charges in Canada, that translates into zero dollars or less at the farm gate in Western Canada.

Now, the reason why the Saudi market is so cheap is because of intense subsidized competition, with U.S. and EEC treasuries fighting it out. In the aftermath of the change in Saudi import policy, trading levels to Saudi Arabia dropped to $55. The Japanese, however, as a so-called rich nation compared to Saudi Arabia, are not eligible for U.S. subsidies. At the very same time as the Saudis are buying barley for about $30 per tonne in Thunder Bay terms, the Japanese are buying barley for about $120 per tonne out of Vancouver. That is the silliness in agriculture today in the world market. The facts are that lower U.S. grain loan rates and the Export Enhancement Program under the U.S. farm bill have pushed Canadian Wheat Board initial prices down well below production costs.

The facts are that the EEC buying price for barley is roughly quadruple today's Canadian Wheat Board initial price, and that is why the U.S. is hitting back. These are the facts. They are not comfortable to deal with, especially for farmers; but they do exist, and they must be addressed. It is not unlike a poker game, and like poker, one's ability to stay in the game depends on the extent of one's bankroll. The stakes are indeed high and the game could be long, perhaps much longer than many people would hope for, unless we squarely face the basics of the issue. These are the real-world stakes at the heart of talking about free trade.

There are ripple effects as well. The fallout from this lack of flexibility in the trade environment is more severe and more widespread than might be suggested at first glance, and it will stay so unless a successful strategy for action can be put in place.

United Grain Growers Limited is confident that the standing committee is aware of the damaging impact of current grain price levels on the western Canadian economy. That has been evidenced by the need for a special Canadian Grains Program on the order of $2.6 billion — I hope you are listening, fellows — and the fact that the western grain stabilization has triggered the largest in history: $1.4 billion.

The dangers extend beyond grain. Low grain prices and tough

grain markets have a habit of increasing livestock production. Poultry, as a regulated industry, is not a viable option for many prospective livestock producers. Overwhelmingly, problems in grain can end up affecting red meat. With Canada's limited population increased red meat production has to find its own markets. These are mainly export markets, particularly to the United States. Canada has already had a taste of what increased export activity in red meats can lead to. Subsidized EEC beef, on one hand, and countervailing duties on Canadian hog exports to the U. S. on the other hand are recent and clear examples of negative impacts on Canadian red meat prices.

As surplus U.S. grain finds its ultimate market as red meat, the sensitivities of U.S. cattle and hog producers will increase. Without the kind of access provided for by the free trade agreement, both western livestock producers and grain growers run the risk of losing an important market outlet. Supplementary or new actions of a tariff, non-tariff, or quota nature are likely to occur if no agreement is in place.

Quite simply, the alternatives to the free trade agreement are not attractive. For western Canada these issues are large. About 20 percent of western beef ends up in the United States. Of every $1.00 flowing back to the hog producer, 40 cents comes from the U.S. market. At a time when no grain market seems secure, we ought to remind ourselves that the biggest single market for western Canadian feed grain is right here in our own livestock industry.

In many parts of the prairies, the fate of grain and livestock are intertwined. The benefits of the market access provisions of the Canada-U.S. agreement will be true benefits to many grain growers as well as livestock producers.

What about charting a course? The board of directors of United Grain Growers Limited submits that Canada is well placed to play a lead role in resolving the trade issues confronting world agriculture today. Indeed, for Canada, it is not a matter of whether we get involved; we must be involved. As the Canada-U.S. free trade agreement recognizes, the major problems facing grain are definitely international in nature.

United Grain Growers Limited strongly urges all Canadian parties involved, including provincial governments and more particularly the Government of Canada, to commit themselves to an assertive and leading role in bringing economic sense back to the world's agricultural markets. This thrust must be cohesive. The dialog must be open-minded and progressive. The approach must be carefully structured. Above all, avoid rhetoric. We can and we must take the initiative. Indeed, we cannot afford not to.

International trade is absolutely vital to the well-being of the western farm economy. Canada sells grain to more than 60 countries in the world. Free markets are absolutely vital to maintaining that market access. Agriculture makes up 10 percent of Canada's total trade and grain picks up the lion's share of that agricultural trade. Without the contribution of grains and oil seeds exports, Canada as a nation would be a net importer of food. In some years, without the export contribution of agriculture, Canada would suffer a merchandise trade deficit.

For the average grain farmer, close to 60 percent of production ends up offshore. No business can survive if the price for 60 percent of production is below cost.

These issues are vital for the survival of the farm community of the West and go to the core of the economic position of Canada as a whole. The bilateral trade agreement between the United States and Canada is a prime example of the kind of leadership that is now required, an example that will not be lost on other countries.

We are deeply concerned about the kind of signal that other countries could get if this Canada-U.S. agreement were to fail. The question will be asked in many capital cities: How in the world can you expect 90-odd countries to agree to something meaningful in Geneva when two countries that have such a close trading relationship cannot?

There are grave dangers for the GATT process if this bilateral deal is not ratified. For agriculture the GATT is critical. I think it is naive to think that backing out of the bilateral agreement will wave a magic wand over the world trade picture and will bring everything to a fresh beginning.

Getting agriculture even on the GATT agenda was an ordeal in itself. The process of demilitarizing agricultural trade is going forward timidly but at least it is going forward. Breaking the Canada-U.S. agreement could shatter this very fragile process to the greatest detriment of agriculture. The downside of breaking the agreement should not be forgotten.

Regarding a way of finding common ground, in stressing the importance of GATT to agriculture — a fact recognized in the bilateral agreement — it would be remiss to not take an opportunity to share some of our thoughts with you about the multilateral negotiation.

As we alluded at the start of this brief, initial agriculture negotiating positions have been tabled at the GATT by several of the major players, including the Europeans. Hopefully a process of identifying common ground will be more mechanical than deciding whether to negotiate. In a GATT forum, finding common ground should simply be a matter of established procedure. Let us all hope it ends up this way.

United Grain Growers is abundantly aware of the fact that negotiation is a very dynamic process. It would be a waste of everyone's time if Canada and special interest groups within Canada viewed trade consultations and hearings such as these as simply an opportunity to air a shopping list of demands.

However, we should not go into GATT negotiations totally unprepared. In reflecting on the issues, UGG's board of directors concluded that we may be of greatest help by offering guidance on broad principles and matters of approach rather than by laying out a detailed road map. We hope that in sharing our thoughts and general direction, we may provide Canada's negotiating team and this committee with a better basis for developing a specific position.

While the goal of having totally free agricultural markets throughout every corner of the world is certainly worthy in theory, it also has to be remembered that the solution to world problems is being forged within an oven of world politics and the pressure cookers of literally dozens of domestic political situations.

Freer markets must be what we aim for. The simplicity of letting everyone do what they do best should not be lost as a goal simply because it currently is not politically possible for all agricultural commodities. Freer markets are better markets for both farmers and consumers. In a recent World Bank study, the income level of farmers worldwide was compared with their level of protection. The upshot was that the better-off farmers tend to be less protected. In the more protected countries, such as Japan, Sweden, and West Germany, consumer prices ironically also tend to be higher.

In our brief to the Saskatchewan Trade Commission in 1986 we proposed an agricultural SALT to end the trade war- a Scheduled Adjustment to Liberalize Trade. This agricultural SALT agreed to at the GATT level could be built upon two basic principles: first, that a country must reduce barriers; and,second, that a country could decide what form that remaining protection ought to take.

The United Grain Growers farmer members have also expressed solid support for the trade deal. At the United Grain Growers annual meeting held in this building in the city on November 3 and 4 of this year, our delegate body of 280 farmers representing 70,000 farmers from across the prairies passed the following resolution:

"Whereas world wide subsidization is having a devastating effect on agriculture in Canada: and whereas Canadian farmers on a large part sell production on a world market and buy inputs on a protected Canadian market; be it resolved that United Grain Growers encourage a free trade policy with the United States and work towards eliminating subsidies worldwide."

We are confident that western Canadian farmers are among the most efficient producers of food in the world. Under conditions where trade barriers are gradually relaxed the most efficient stand to reap the greatest benefits. We have quality products, we have world class handling and grading systems, and we have developed a reputation in the world as an honest and reliable broker in the agricultural trade arena.

In a sense, agriculture is a model of all that is good and bad with world trade. On the bad side, there are all kinds of truly stupid distortions that can happen. Does it make sense, for instance, for Caribbean countries on the edge of bankruptcy to be excluded from selling sugar in the U.S. market? Should a country as rich as Japan protect its rice farmers by paying them six times the world price? The cost to all of us in the world is simply too high.

Another example of the bad side of agriculture is an extra cost of $900 U.S. per European family coupled with a loss of one million net manufacturing jobs in the EEC. The bad side is that consumer food costs in Japan are 60 percent above the levels that would prevail under a freer trade arrangement.

We must keep in mind the good side also. The good side is that Canadians enjoy some of the cheapest and highest quality food in the world. Agriculture, rather than being a laggard, is now actually leading other industries in how to tackle protectionism on a world-wide basis. The elements of the Canada-U.S. free trade agreement are far too important to be confined to the extremes of partisan politics or nationalistic ideologies.

In our opinion the elements of this agreement are consistent with the long term goals of dismantling barriers to trade. The agreement also respects Canada's obligations under GATT. It is our opinion that the elements are sound, are in the farmer's interest, our industry's interest and the national interest.

Chapter nineteen:
our trade problem with U.S.
isn't their laws but their courts

Alan M. Rugman

Mr. Rugman is Professor of International Business, University of Toronto. From a submission to the House of Commons standing committee on external affairs and international trade, Toronto, December 7, 1987.

The Canada-United States free trade agreement of October 1987 signals profound changes in bilateral economic relations. The new trade policy outlined in the elements of the agreement offers both opportunities and challenges for all Canadians.

Basically, I believe there are economic opportunities and political challenges. In my 20 years as an economics and management professor it has become clear to me that Canada cannot afford to ignore the realities of international trade and investment. In my judgment, the free trade agreement is a major step forward for Canada. It is the right agreement at the right price at the right time.

I hope its clear economic advantages will not be lost by short-term political considerations.

Rather than review my previous writings on the need for bilateral trade agreement, let me illustrate this point by developing my thoughts on two key aspects of the actual agreement, dispute settlement and investment issues.

Over the last seven years the United States has developed a system of administered protection. American producers have used the countervailing duty and anti-dumping provisions of U.S. trade law as a weapon of competitive strategy aimed at foreign, including Canadian, corporations. The quasi-judicial nature of the current process of U.S. trade law hearings and investigations is biased in favor of U.S. plaintiffs and against Canadian exporters. The operation of the system is decentralized and its use is often in conflict with official U.S. trade policy. The result is what some of us have called a form of administered protection which denies Canada secure access to the vital U.S. market.

From Canada's viewpoint the bilateral trade agreement required an effective method to stop the abusive nature of U.S. trade law procedures. The current problems of U.S. trade law stem from the process by which investigations are made. The U.S. International Trade Commission and the U.S. Commerce Department no longer pursue technical track investigations; instead, their investigations have become politicized. The free trade agreement of October 1987 is the first step towards resolving these problems.

Since the 1979 U.S. Trade Act made this type of administered protection possible, there have been more than 300 separate countervailing duty cases and about 400 anti-dumping cases in the United States. A number of these, approximately 30, have affected Canadian agriculture, resource, and manufactured exports. The well-known cases included live swine and pork, fish, raspberries, carnation flowers, softwood lumber, potash and steel.

An increasing proportion of these cases, about 70 percent, result in positive preliminary determinations of material injury — a decision made by the ITC — and a substantial proportion, more than 30 percent, result in penalties being imposed to offset alleged foreign subsidies. This aggressive use of U.S. trade law procedures has created great difficulties for many Canadian individuals and corporations exporting to the United States, particularly in our resource-based regions.

Much of the process of investigation and adjudication is automatic and decentralized to producer interests. This leaves relatively little scope for the direction of trade policy by either the President or Congress. Instead, these two branches of U.S. government are frequently in conflict about the nature of trade policy.

This results in an institutional context closer to anarchy than to efficient international trade policy making and execution. With no practical safeguards for the national interest, and given the limited power of consumers and the executive, the current administration of trade law in the United States encourages mercantilist tendencies and threatens the welfare of both the country and its trading partners.

It is apparent to me that the Canadian side in the free trade negotiations with the United States made considerable progress towards resolving this problem by insisting on a form of binding dispute settlement mechanism. From January 1, 1989, Canada will have a legally binding appeals mechanism which can be used to offset abusive U.S. trade law procedures

How this binational tribunal works in practice will depend upon the cases referred to it. The mere existence of the tribunal should deter frivolous and dubious U.S. petitions. Through this mechanism Canada has achieved its primary objective of securing access to the U.S. market.

The breakthrough in terms of international trade law is that in the free trade agreement Canada has obtained, for the first time in history, a legally binding and effective method of resolving trade disputes with the United States. Canada has achieved a system whereby the results of the trade law actions can be reviewed by a binational panel, and Canada's rights to protest the abuses of U.S. trade laws have been established.

Now there is a mechanism for Canada to influence and potentially reverse the questionable investigative practices of the U.S. International Trade Commission and the U.S. Commerce Department in their gathering of data and analysis. This statement assumes that the Canadian negotiators are correct in saying that the economic evidence can be reviewed by the binational panel, a point that has been supported in recent legal opinions.

With the dispute settlement provisions of the elements in place, it is highly likely that the October 1986 Commerce Department decision on softwood lumber would have been overturned on appeal to this new binational panel. The reversal of the Commerce Department's 1983 decision on general availability reflected political rather than technical-track reasons.

Also, it is likely in my opinion, that the standing in the recent anti-dumping case on potash would have been denied to the U.S. petitioners upon appeal to the proposed binational panel. The reason is that the two U.S. petitioners had only three percent of the U.S. market for potash. Similarly, the views of processors and other intermediate users of resource-based products are now likely to be heard by the new binational panel, provided that their information is placed on the record such that evidence can be reviewed in a judicial review by the binational panel.

In the case of the fresh Atlantic ground fish dispute of 1985 to 1986, the desires of U.S. processors and U.S. consumers to have access to cheap Canadian fish may have led to a different outcome in the countervail if a binational panel had recognized their standing.

Inevitably, the panel will bring greater objectivity to the process of investigation, even under existing U.S. trade law.

Canada still needs to work to obtain an even more effective bilateral investigative body over the next five to seven years. This will be done under the clause in the trade agreement calling for "the development of a substitute system of laws in both countries for anti-dumping and countervailing duties. In this "substitute regime" we will need to distinguish between acceptable and unacceptable industrial subsidies. But this is not a one-way street.

While Canada has regional development and other generally available subsidies there are similar subsidies in the United States. So if Canadian subsidies in these areas are removed, it would only be in return for the removal of U.S. direct and indirect subsidies in such industries as agriculture and defence.

In practice, in my opinion it is doubtful that much progress will be made in removing either Canadian or American subsidies. In that case the "interim" dispute-settlement mechanism may well become permanent, perhaps not a bad outcome for Canada. The bilateral dispute settlement procedure outlined in the elements represents such a vast improvement over the abuse of existing U.S. trade law procedures that it is of significant benefit to Canada.

In a world of global competition and triad power, ready and secure access to the U.S. market remains the basic requirement for Canada's future well being. The free trade agreement moves Canada towards attainment of this long-run economic goal by providing increased opportunities for access to the U.S. market, defended by a legally binding dispute-settlement mechanism.

To finally resolve the problem of U.S. trade law procedures, Canada has to continue to make the running by developing constituencies in the United States which begin to recognize the abusive nature of the administrations of U.S. trade laws and the costs to the United States of this type of invisible protectionism.

Finally, on this topic, let me re-emphasize a point made earlier in this debate; namely, that regional development programs are at risk under the status quo. If, as Mr. John Turner advocated yesterday, the free trade agreement is rejected, then the Atlantic provinces will find that most subsidies and other regional development programs will remain subject to U.S. countervail and anti-dumping actions. Yet in the free trade agreement, the integrity of such programs was guaranteed because they were specifically exempted.

In addition, the binational panel would safeguard such programs on the remote chance that they were still subject to U.S. countervail, since the Canadians on the tribunal would be able to demonstrate that our regional development programs are generally available internal transfer payments rather than specific export subsidies.

In terms of foreign direct investment, critics of the free trade agreement use the thinking of the 1960s rather than the facts of the 1980s. At that time, foreign ownership of the Canadian economy was a legitimate concern. However, in the last 10 years, Canadian direct investment has been growing at over 20 percent a year. By 1985 the stock of Canadian-owned investment in the United States was $35 billion, about 60 percent of the value of the U.S. stock in Canada.

At these rates of growth, there will soon be as much Canadian investment in the United States as there is American investment in Canada. Canada stands to benefit from the national treatment provision of the trade deal just as much as the Americans. In my opinion, this was not a concession to the United States, but a sensible move by our trade negotiators to retain Canadian access to the U.S. market at a time when future U.S. restrictions on inward investment are almost inevitable. This method of securing access to the American market for Canadian investment complements the secure access for Canadian exports achieved in the trade deal.

Chapter twenty:
U.S. uranium mines won't be allowed to shut the door on Canada

L.G. Bonar

Mr. Bonar is chairman and chief executive office of Eldorado Nuclear Limited. From a submission to the House of Commons standing committee on external afairs and international trade, Ottawa, Dec. 1, 1987.

Canada is the only country that mines, processes and exports uranium. Therefore, our industry is a unique source of supply for electric utilities around the world. The five uranium mines (two in Ontario and three in Saskatchewan), plus Eldorado's uranium processing operations in Ontario (Blind River and Port Hope), generate combined export revenue of approximately $1 billion annually.

Saskatchewan's three mines supply more uranium than any other producing region in the world. In recent years, this has been a source of pride in Saskatchewan and a cause of concern in the United States, the largest uranium market anywhere.

The reason for the discontent south of the border is quite simple. The U.S. uranium industry has lost its position as the largest in the world. After years of operating within the safe confines of a market protected from foreign competition by U.S. government policy, American companies have had to compete with non-U.S. producers in a fierce battle for market share and survival. Many mines have been lost in the struggle.

U.S. uranium mining companies have seen their production drop from 39 million pounds of U08 in 1981 to 10 million pounds this year. They are the victims of the high-cost mines which rely on low-grade uranium deposits.

Meanwhile, the Canadians have been selling more and more uranium into the U.S. market, in large part because Saskatchewan has some of the largest, most accessible and highest-grade uranium deposits anywhere. In contrast with U.S. mines, Saskatchewan producers have seen their production rise from 7.5 million pounds in 1981 to 18 million this year.

While the U.S. share of world production dropped from 34 percent to 11 percent, Saskatchewan's share has tripled to 19 percent.

The U.S. industry sees only one solution to its problems — stop the Canadians. They have worked the U.S. courts and Congress with this objective in mind and with considerable success. Fortunately, U.S. electric utilities which use Canadian uranium and the U.S. Administration recognize that protection is an unfair, indirect tax on the consumer.

The Canada-U.S. free trade agreement repudiates the idea that U.S. residential and industrial consumers of electricity should be forced into subsidizing U.S. uranium mines.

Passage of the agreement by Parliament and Congress will mark a watershed in the history of Canada's uranium industry. It will guarantee that competition in the world's largest uranium market will be judged only on commercial terms. In effect, the agreement represents a Bill of Rights for Canada's exporters.

What does this mean for Saskatchewan? At a minimum, it secures the present.

Today, the uranium industry is one of the largest employers in the province and it is the largest source of employment in northern Saskatchewan. In total, some 6,000 residents of this province either work in our industry or are employed because of it. Almost half of Saskatchewan's 1987 uranium production, which is the foundation of this employment, was sold to utilities in the United States. Securing these existing jobs is a major accomplishment.

Eldorado is the largest producer and seller of uranium, not only in Saskatchewan but in North America. Because we have been in this business longer than anyone, we have a world-wide customer base and are therefore less dependent on the U.S. market than some other companies. Nonetheless, closure of the U.S. market to foreign producers such as ourselves would have drastic consequences for Eldorado's 1,000 employees in Canada and for the company as a whole.

This year we will achieve a substantial financial recovery, going from a loss of $64.4 million last year to, hopefully, a break-even or a slight profit in 1987. Exclusion from the U.S. market would have driven us in the opposite direction.

Maintaining the present benefits of this industry is vital but the Canada-U.S. agreement has the potential to do much more for the country's uranium mining industry. If the forces of supply and demand are allowed to work, employment, production, sales and provincial revenues will continue to grow well into the 1990s.

Several companies are proposing major development projects which could lead to the investment of hundreds of millions of dollars in northern Saskatchewan within five years.

For example, Eldorado is proposing to bring another three ore bodies into production at our Rabbit Lake operations. They would be developed in phases, influenced as much as anything by market conditions. They represent a capital investment of more than $100 million and will extend the life of our existing operations well into the next century.

We estimate our Rabbit Lake operations will generate direct expenditures of approximately $3.5 billion between 1992 and 2012, the 20 years during which these new mines are expected to operate.

Fully two-thirds of those funds will be spent in Saskatchewan, on capital investments; the purchase of local products and services to support our operations; on salaries and benefits to our 400 employees in Saskatchewan, and on provincial taxes and royalties.

What we are proposing represents $2.3 billion of expenditures in Saskatchewan's future. Remembering that others in the industry also have expansion plans, your committee can understand why the Canada-U.S. free trade agreement is so strongly supported by the uranium industry.

The agreement will not guarantee that these investments are made and that this growth and income potential is realized. But it forcefully removes a major uncertainty facing all of us — the very real prospect of new barriers to trade with our biggest uranium customer.

In addition to the trade agreement's implications for Canada's uranium mines, the proposal also deals with the processing of uranium. Successive Canadian governments, dating back to the late 1950s, have held the view that Canadian uranium should be processed before it is exported. The policy has been reviewed and amended frequently in recent years with the primary objective of ensuring that it doesn't penalize those utilities which buy uranium from Canadian mines and therefore doesn't hinder the industry's exports. For example, foreign utilities are not expected to pay more, to wait longer or to abrogate foreign processing contracts and thereby incur large financial penalties just because Canada wants its uranium processed domestically.

The bottom line of the policy, however, is that **if Canadian processing is generally competitive,** Canadian uranium should be processed before export. This "bottom line" principle is consistent with provincial mining Acts in Ontario, Manitoba, and Saskatchewan, and for decades it has been fundamental to how Canadians view their resource industries.

Earlier this year, Eldorado recommended to the Government of Canada's trade negotiators that U.S. utilities be given a blanket exemption to Canada's further processing policy. We did this for several reasons.

First, free access of Canadian mine production to the U.S. market represented a major opportunity and would shield Canadian companies, such as ourselves, from the wave of American protectionism.

Second, our two U.S. processing competitors want to process

Canadian uranium and persuaded many in Congress to impose a tariff of more than 100 percent on Eldorado processing because of Canada's policy. This proposed retaliation, plus the threat of a uranium embargo, impaired our company's ability to sell processing services in the U.S.

Third, our U.S. competitors, unlike those in Europe, are owned in the private sector and, therefore, the utility customer is under less pressure to purchase processing from sources within its country. Because U.S. utilities are free to purchase processing services from anyone and because of our close proximity to the U.S., Eldorado believed that it would still be allowed to compete on equal terms in the U.S. processing market.

The strategy of giving up the processing policy for Canadian uranium consumed by U.S. utilities has succeeded in assuring our mining industry's access to the largest nuclear energy market in the world.

Quite apart from this major consideration, the Canada-U.S. free trade agreement, once approved by both countries, will encourage consumers, whether companies or individuals, to think in terms of North American sources of supply. Some utilities will continue their practice of "Buy American." In our opinion, however, many more utilities will continue or start to "Buy North American." By fostering new attitudes, the agreement helps open up new opportunities for Canadian processing.

Can Eldorado's Ontario operations compete in this commercial environment?

The company has always had to be competitive in order to process Canadian uranium. During the last five years, our processing volume has doubled despite a highly competitive world market.

However, the trade agreement does put more pressure on Eldorado. If we matched our competition in the past, the federal government decided who would get the business. If we match our competition in the future, the U.S. utility will decide. Therefore, to maintain our existing business and make it grow, Eldorado will have to be decisively competitive.

The company has invested $300 million in new processing facilities at Blind River and Port Hope since 1982. They feature the most advanced technology in the industry and employ a highly skilled workforce.

Eldorado will continue to demonstrate its ability to compete. In our opinion, exempting U.S. utility customers from Canada's processing policy does not threaten our workforce in Ontario. On the contrary, our objective is growth, not the status quo.

PART FIVE:
THE DOMESTIC POLITICS
OF PROTECTION
AND TRADE

Chapter twenty one:
the alternative to free trade
is a controlled economy

J.A. Gordon Bell

Mr. Bell is deputy chairman and president, Scotiabank. from an address to the Canadian Club of Toronto, October 26, 1987.

The issues we face include:

One, we are in the process of redefining our economic relationship with the United States. It is a cliche to say so but it is nonetheless true that there is no external relationship that is more important to our national well being than this one.

Two, we are in the process of redesigning — again — our basic constitutional arrangements. There is nothing more fundamental to the shape of a country's future than its constitution.

And three, in my industry, lately banking but now the full gamut of financial services, we have already broken patterns of financial activity that go back decades. There is very little as basic to the economic well being of every Canadian as the structure and quality of our financial industry.

Quite an agenda, wouldn't you say?

If we are going to get the decisions right, however, the first thing we had better do is get the debate right. Unfortunately, we are having the wrong debate.

On trade, for example, we are hearing a cacophony from interest groups each asserting its own claim to protection from the impact of the more open economic relationship now in prospect with the United States. And, as Al Jolson would have put it, you ain't heard nothin' yet.

Now I think that various interests are understandably concerned, be those interests unions, economic sectors, industries, or social groups. What is at stake for these groups is not simply benefits — benefits that have been laid onto our economy over the decades like slices of salami on a baguette, at considerable cost to consumers, taxpayers, economic productivity, and government revenues, I might add. What is at stake is power — or more precisely, the prospect that many groups will lose their power to pressure government to intervene on their behalf against the interest of other, less-organized groups.

The reason many economic and other interests will lose power is very simply that government will lose power to intervene on behalf of one group versus another because interventionist instruments such as tariffs, quotas, regulations, subsidies, administrative actions, etc., will be proscribed or limited under the Canada-U.S. agreement.

Is that good or bad for the country? I suppose we all have views — and I think it is good for the country — but I suggest to you that it is the wrong debate. The debate we need is not about whether we should protect one group or another from having to adjust to changes in the world economy. Indeed, if we ever needed an object lesson in that, we got it last week [with the collapse of stock market prices]. There is no such thing as real protection. For all the illusion of protection, I don't know anybody who wasn't hurt in some way by last week's events.

The debate we need now is about how we can encourage and facilitate adjustment. Adapting to world competition is absolutely essential to our continuing prosperity.

Building national wealth is necessary to sustain a country that is strong, free, confident in its identity and possessing the wealth to make the choices that are the essence of a sovereign state and a sovereign people.

As to the risks out there, sure we're going to take some hits but nothing like the kicking we'll take if we try to pretend we don't have to compete. That is the message the markets are giving us. We ignore it at our peril.

Now consider the debate on the constitution. The arguments over the Meech Lake Accord seem to me, equally to miss the point. That debate is again dominated by the concern of various interest groups, about federal-provincial power, about how various social and other groups will be affected.

The fact is that decisions on social programs are also economic decisions. Social policies affect economic performance and personal well being, both in terms of direct benefits and indirect costs. They affect tax rates, government deficits, costs to business, the income that individuals have to spend. This particular set of changes may well serve to make differing social policies in different provinces instruments of inter-provincial economic competition. If only for that, the Meech Lake Accord bears on our economic position in the world.

But the Meech Lake Accord will bear on our world position in other ways.

Let me give you a precise example of what I mean. In 1824 the U.S. Supreme Court struck down a New York State law preventing a steamboat service between New York and New Jersey. This decision

The hidden agenda

Don MacCharles, *professor of economics, University of New Brunswick, Saint John. Excerpt from article in Financial Post, January 8, 1988..*

And this gets us around to the main issue of the debate, which is not about free trade at all, but about whether politicians in this country will have the power to intervene in markets for idiosyncratic reasons related to their views on industrial and social policies. The left-leaning politicians in particular are concerned, since a country that has markets freely and competitively setting prices and allocating resources cannot have interventionist policies and remain both economically viable in the longer term and avoid countervails and other sanctions by its trading partners. The free trade deal clearly will limit the ability of interventionist-minded politicians to implement their social agendas and that is why [Joseph] Ghiz [Premier of Prince Edward Island], Ontario Premier David Peterson, NDP Leader Ed Broadbent, and United Autoworkers President Bob White, among others, are against it.

prevented state impediments to interstate commerce and ensured the development of the United States as the world's wealthiest economy. Justice Oliver Wendell Holmes later said it secured the survival of the United States.

In Canada, alas, we have done things differently — often indeed, whatever the wisdom of it, for the sake of doing things differently from Americans. So our economy, aside from being layered with benefits to particular economic and social interests, is also piled up with inter-provincial barriers of all kinds.

I know that Canada has different problems and we have to solve them in our own way. But I would advance the radical proposition that we do not have to be stupid about it....

The Canadian financial industry, in less than a year, has been fundamentally and irrevocably realigned. But even now regulators are still lagging the change and delays in necessary legislative reform sees us still having to chase the competition.

Imagine where this country's financial industry would be today had we not wasted interminable time debating how to divvy up the take within Canada and, instead, produced the first Big Bang and not the second or third or fourth. It is being there first that commands the premium. We could have been a leader in this. Instead, we were a follower. This way of being Canadian is no longer enough. The world is moving too fast.

Having suddenly re-oriented ourselves to the world financial market — a very important achievement, even if late — we remain burdened by certain aspects of our navel-gazing past. It is puzzling, for example, that banks will not be able to sell insurance directly to their customers through branch systems. That we are not permitted to engage in the leasing of automobiles. In light of the Canada-U.S. free trade agreement which opens Canadian banking fully to U.S. competition, it does not seem prudent to prevent Canadian banks from selling data-processing services — an area of particular strength in the industry — while Americans will be allowed to do so.

Given the competition we now face, all Canadian institutions need a playing field that is level with the world's, or preferably gives us an advantage. We aren't there yet.

More troubling, however, is that we are being dragged back into that most traditional and Canadian of debates, where to draw the line between federal and provincial regulatory responsibilities. We do not need this kind of debate. We do not need it because in 120 years as a country, we have never been able to resolve the question either to anyone's satisfaction or with any degree of permanence. We do not need it, more importantly, because — while federal and provincial governments resume the argument about how to carve up power over the financial industry — world financial markets see us as comparatively handicapped players.

If being Canadian is to miss the point, we are truly a nation of patriots. This way of being Canadian is clearly not enough.

But here we go again with the wrong debate.

The objective must be to see that we can cut the mustard competitively in global markets. That is the debate we need. What do we have to do? What do we have to avoid?

Let me take a stab at some answers, mainly by reference to the trade issue. I choose trade because the Constitution, I think, is a done deal, and what applies to trade in general applies to financial services in particular.

All of us have watched the drama of the past few weeks. I do not

146

know any better than anyone else how it is going to turn out.

If Congress and Parliament approve the agreement, however, we will have acquired two significant instruments for advancing our prosperity. One is a carrot, the other a stick. The carrot, of course, is the lower-risk opportunities that the United States market will present as a result of the trade agreement. I say lower risk rather than secure, because the last thing anyone would call the U.S. market is risk free. The stick is the healthy discipline that easier U.S. access to our market will impose on Canadian business.

The NDP alternative

Excerpts from an editorial in the Globe and Mail, January 22, 1988.

"The New Democratic Party would tear up Canada's free trade agreement with the United States, discourage deregulation, privatization and foreign investment, control energy prices, increase the use of tax breaks and state procurement to influence corporate behavior and expand public ownership. This comes naturally to a socialist party which, as the New Democrats' Trade Option paper says, 'is frankly interventionists'..."

"The NDP would combat regional unemployment with 'tax incentives, grants or other subsidies' to industrial projects that meet local procurement targets. In sum, there would be more state intervention and higher interprovincial trade barriers.

"... the NDP would seek 'a much lower level' for interest rates through orders to the Bank of Canada. This, says the NDP, would 'secure productive investment in Canada' rather than drive it away. There is no mention of the effect on the Canadian dollar, which would fall; on inflation, which would rise; or on the ability of Canadians to borrow abroad, which would weaken. There is no mention of public deficits or debt, or any recognition of their relationship to economic growth and employment."

... the NDP offers an alternative — socialist, protectionist and palpably inferior to the present course of Canadian economic policy."

Both carrot and stick will present us with tough decisions but, on balance, I believe they will accelerate our adjustment to a better competitive position in the world economy, not just the U.S. economy. But the extent to which — and, indeed, whether — they enhance our position in the world and our prosperity will depend on the actions we take. Nothing is guaranteed.

The tougher decisions will come if the agreement is not approved. That the U.S. Congress might not approve the agreement is at least a possibility. What then?

We will be in a highly dangerous position but not necessarily because of U.S. protectionism, which has not been exactly benign in terms of Canada these last couple of years. Even under the trade agreement we have, it seems likely, to have a fair bit of sting left. Nor, the rhetoric not withstanding, is it because the status quo is untenable. The fact is that over the past 15 years we have been jerked around pretty well by oil prices, inflation, interest rates, deflation, recession, etc. We may not like it but we can live without it if we have to.

By far the greater danger is political. What will endanger our prospects is not the U.S. Congress rejecting this agreement. It is how we respond should the agreement be rejected. The fact is that the trade initiative has been the centre piece of a whole range of market-oriented policies, including but not confined to financial industry reform, freer foreign investment flows, increased (then reduced) capital gains exemptions, privatization of certain Crown corporations, tax reform, and so on.

Succeed or fail, the mere fact that the initiative was made has had some very positive effects. A good deal of adjustment, expansion and realignment has gone on throughout the economy in anticipation of an agreement. The changes in the financial industry are only the most obvious examples. The fact is, we have a private sector that is now better geared up for external competition. Win, lose or draw in the U.S. Congress, this has improved the operation of our economy.

The second positive effect has been on federal-provincial relations. Up until the recession of 1982, we had an economy that was becoming increasingly more balkanized. For example, recall that Alberta decided not to provide petrochemical feedstocks to Sarnia. Certain provinces barred out-of-province workers on construction projects. Truckloads of tomatoes were stopped at the Ontario-Quebec border because they had been weighed in kilograms rather than pounds.

Since 1984 the premiers, singularly concentrated on the Canada-U.S. issue, have cooled out many of these go-it-alone provincial impulses of the 1970s and early 1980s. Perhaps the effect was somewhat akin to the prospect of hanging, politically and economically, if due attention was not paid to the issue. As the saying goes, the prospect of the noose has a remarkable effect in concentrating the mind.

But what happens if there is no approval of the agreement? What happens if the noose, which has kept the provinces and federal government alike concentrated on trade issues, is no longer there and there is no longer the need to hang together? The great danger then is that we will hang separately.

By and large, the opponents of freer trade hold an interventionist view. If they block the deal, I think they will seek much more vigorous use of subsidies, quotas, regulations, governmental decisions as to winners and losers — all those government instruments that the free trade agreement would proscribe.

The federal government will be hard pressed to resist. In any case, you can bet your sinking dollar the opposition parties will come on hard with interventionist policies if the government doesn't. And they might well be elected on such a platform. That is one way we can hang separately.

But a greater danger may be that rejection of this agreement will send the provinces scattering to their own independent economic policies, the increased use of inter-provincial barriers, a new balkanization of our already fragmented economy, and the shattering of national purpose at the precise time it is most required. And, I fear that our new constitution would encourage that fragmentation.

Well, as I said, we Canadians have our own ways. And while we don't have to be stupid about it, the danger is that we will be. The danger is that our governments will do some damn fool thing that will leave us worse off than need be.

Let me conclude with a bit of history. Being Canadian is being a beneficiary of the vision and political will of past leaders of this country.

Sir John A. Macdonald was not only the principal architect of this country's rise from colony to nation. The economic infrastructure and programs known as the National Policy were also a part of his vision, and it does not deny his contribution to say that, more than a century later, they need to be replaced by policies that reach out to the world. Sir Wilfrid Laurier presided over the opening of Canada's west and, through his policies, one of the greatest periods of growth and expansion in the country's history. William Lyon MacKenzie King seized the opportunity of war time and, with C.D. Howe, transformed Canada from a rural to an industrial economy. Louis St. Laurent and Lester Pearson established the sinews of a country capable of sustaining and developing its human resources — national medicare, pensions, post-secondary education, and the like. Pierre Trudeau brought home the Constitution, established the Charter of Rights and resolved, for a time anyway, the question of Quebec's place in Canada.

These were men of vision who lived in times that demanded vision.

We live in a comparable time. We have a comparable need. I think that, whatever one might think of the trade agreement, the present government will be credited by history with having a vision of a Canada ready to compete in the world. Now, the government must have the political will to sustain that vision and, if the route to a more competitive economy through freer trade with the U.S. is closed, to find another road going in the same direction. But others require vision too — we here in this room. We must have the vision to compete in the world because it is on our capacity to do so, and our willingness to do so, that Canada's future prosperity depends.

If our vision is lacking, then the hills and valleys beyond the horizon will be rugged indeed. But if it is there and if we have the will to compete then the future is ours to shape. And if you and I do well along the way we will have no reason to be other than proud.

Chapter twenty-two:
The rape of the National Energy Program will never happen again

Peter Lougheed

Mr. Lougheed is a former Premier of Alberta. From a submission to the House of Commons standing commiittee on external affairs and international relations, Ottawa, November 18, 1987.

What I hope we are debating in the country today is the issue of jobs for young people. I respect both points of views and it is an important debate for Canada, but it really is going to be a question of the future of our country, not tomorrow, not five years or perhaps ten years from now, but about the jobs for our young people. We will have different points of view and that is fine. I welcome it.

You know that jobs come from the private sector. I wear a different hat than the last few times I have been in Ottawa. Now I am in the private sector rather than the public sector. I always argued that if you want to talk about job creation there has to be stimulating investment. What is stimulating investment? It is getting an entrepreneur to make a decision to commit his or her funds to job expansion within Canada and the various regions of Canada.

I have had a chance, as a premier of Alberta for 14 years and in the private sector for two years, to have a fairly broad exposure in my travels. I have travelled a lot in the Pacific Rim, in the European economic community and other places.

I have had an opportunity to observe Canada's competitiveness and it always surprises me that whether it is a rancher in Alberta, a fisherman in Newfoundland or an auto worker in Ontario, we can be confident about our degree of competitiveness and productivity. I think in the last number of years we have worked pretty hard at that.

When I first got involved in this issue, about the fall of 1984, there were three options for Canada and our trade relationship with the U.S. We could stay with the status quo, go into a sectoral approach like the Auto Pact or we could approach it on a comprehensive basis. I thought a lot about it before making my first presentation to the First Minister's Conference in Regina in February of 1985.

I felt that the status quo was fooling ourselves because I did not think then and do not think today that we can turn back and think about our trade relationship in years past. It is too dynamic and it has changed too much.

What about sectorally? I think it is a pretty difficult decision. I do not think it will fly; I do not think it could get off the ground. I know some of you have a different view about it.

I felt that a comprehensive agreement under article 24 of the GATT was the right way to go. I looked at the October 3 agreement. No agreement is perfect. I have been involved in negotiating a number of public sector agreements, but I really feel good about this one.

The real surprise to me was energy. I did not expect an agreement as comprehensive overall as it was or an agreement that had such an impact in terms of energy.

It is not a perfect agreement, but I have never seen one that was. It is a great launching pad for our entrepreneurs, if you think about it. It is a launching pad because as our entrepreneurs develop their organizations and their companies within a North American environment, much more than today, they will be able to move out into the Pacific Rim with strength, vitality and confidence. It is a stage, as I see it. I see the 1990s as a stage in which we are going to be launching entrepreneurs in the North American environment. I see after that moving from this base on a worldwide basis in the Pacific Rim in particular. I do not think I exaggerate when I feel that in my travels and my experience, for western Canada this is not only positive but also a must.

The key, the real win-win of the agreement, is in energy. It is there really in such a substantial way, in my opinion, because it is going to encourage investment not only in the conventional oil and gas side but in the oil sands and the heavy oils. I would like to explain the reasons. Basically, the situation is that we now export one-third of our natural gas and one-third of our crude oil to the United States. Sustaining and expanding that market are essential to new investment. The Canadian market for both oil and natural gas is not large enough to attract the new investment we need and can accommodate.

The biggest plus of this agreement is it could preclude a federal government from bringing in a National Energy Program ever again. That means something to somebody who has been involved in $60 billion skimmed off the top of what the market price was and transferred to central Canada: $60 billion is what the National Energy Program rape amounted to.

You say those are strong words. Not to me. Not to the Canadian drillers. Not to the entrepreneurs affected by that.

Well, you cannot do it if this deal comes through. Let us put that right on the table. Those who want to have another NEP , fine. But you cannot do it, because you cannot put a made-in-Canada price that takes $27-a-barrel oil and forces it down to $18 again. We will go with the market, up and down.We lived with a down market in 1986. We will have down markets again. But we will take the marketplace. This agreement forces the marketplace to decide on the pricing. I think that is a very big positive. It is sure as heck a positive to the investor.

In the U.S. it is important, because what happens when — and I think it is "when", not "if" — the Americans get involved with importing over 50 percent of their crude oil requirements? Well, there is going to be a move in the U.S. to put on an oil import tax. There is going to be a move to restrict those foreign imports. There is going to be a move to work in ways that make them less dependent upon the Persian Gulf. But guess what? Under this agreement, Canada is not going to be part of those import restrictions. Canada is going to be part of an arrangement for supply and not looked at on a foreign supply basis. That could be in the mid-1990s. It could be a very major factor. But talking to investors, it is one they have in their minds.

What about oil sands? If you look at oil sands, from my experience the impact comes from the decision of the investor. First, he is going to look at his forecast on price. Secondly, he is going to look at his cost factor. But primarily he is going to say, I do not have to worry about my market...oh, unless I hit a situation after I have spent those billions of dollars where a federal government tells me I cannot export that product.

Well, I think an investor, if this agreement goes through — I do not "think", I sense more than think — is going to be very much encouraged by an agreement like this to risk billions of dollars in oil sands and heavy oil projects. You ask why — why is this so great in Alberta? Why in the heck can they not do it in Oklahoma and Texas? I will tell you. There are three major reasons. We have lower finding costs in the oil and gas business in Canada than they have in the U.S. That is a big plus for an investor. Secondly, they have drilled their country out on land almost exclusively. We have better geological prospects in the frontier areas, in the northern part of British Columbia and the northern part of Alberta, onshore and in the territories. We have the geological prospects they do not have. Two big reasons, if I am an investor and I want to be in Canada if this agreement goes through. And finally, there is just a superb group of technical people and drillers and service people in this country who can make it hum and increase the activity. We have the capacity, and they are Canadian-owned companies that have shown ability to export it.

So I could see in the mid-1990s, with this agreement, a situation where energy for North America, coming out of Canada — all parts of Canada, not just Alberta — would create a tremendous engine for jobs once again. If we do not go ahead with this deal, it will be very sad in terms of the flight of capital. If you have looked at the figures on the flight of capital after the National Energy Program, $11 billion left Canada when the National Energy Program came in. That is an incredible figure.

It is a crossroads decision. I am glad there is a good debate. It is terrific. I welcome it and I intend to be as much a part of it as I can as a private citizen. I am sure it is going to get emotional, just like I am emotional about it. That is okay. I do not think Canadians are going to be neutral on this. By the time it comes down, everybody is going to have an opinion. It may or may not be informed, but they are going to have one.

What does it come down to? It really comes down to the question of what we think about ourselves. I think the average citizen, when he has to make a final view on this, whether it is May, June, or July of next year, is going to come down to that particular point: do I have confidence in myself, my neighbors, and my country to compete with Tacoma, with Atlanta, with Des Moines, with Houston? Do I have confidence?

I will tell you where the young people are going to come from. They are going to come overwhelmingly yes. That is where the debate will come down to, and I am glad I am on the side of confidence because what this country can do and the entrepreneurs can do is compete.

I will not get any more emotional. I will stop and take your questions.

Chapter twenty-three
the bias of a left-leaning media

Robert M. MacIntosh

Mr. MacIntosh is president of the Canadian Bankers' Association. This article first appeared in the Toronto Star, January 18, 1988.

The cultural community and the political left have been reinforcing each other in the debate over the Canada-U.S. free trade deal.

Since many writers and broadcasters are themselves part of a cultural community that is somewhat politically left, there is a heavy bias in our media against the free trade deal.

Even in relatively conservative publications, the selection of stories by reporters, and their treatment by headline writers and editors, gives a very disproportionate weight to the opponents of free trade.

The CBC has been churning out a steady diet of hostile news stories and commentaries by the nationalists, union leaders and the minority of businessmen who are opposed.

On two successive mornings recently, the CBC featured Ontario NDP leader Bob Rae commenting on a conference in Washington, but made no mention of the views of the numerous Canadians there who supported the free trade deal.

CBC Radio gave almost no coverage to the important news conference on free trade organized by the Business Council on National Issues, which featured Donald Macdonald and Peter Lougheed.

The attitude of the cultural and communications community is very hard to understand, given the fact that our cultural institutions were almost entirely excluded from the free trade negotiations.

In my opinion, the Canadian negotiators were right to exclude our cultural industries from the bargaining process, not only because it would have made a deal impossible, but because it was the right thing to do.

What gives this country unity, to the extent we have any, is a common bond of ideas and beliefs, a shared political and social history, and a growing identity of values that are different from those of the Americans. To preserve and enhance those values, it is necessary to protect our cultural institutions from the economics of the U.S. mass media.

But the free trade deal does this! So why is the cultural-communications industry hostile nevertheless? In my opinion, there are several elements that come together to explain it.

First, there is the leftward political bias of the cultural-communications industry, which can, therefore, see no good in the deal even if the deal is a good one.

The media have a responsibility to provide Canadians with not just criticism, but in-depth analysis. There is little of the latter.

Second, there is the factor of technical competence. An overwhelming number of professional Canadian economists support the free trade deal, but the media have a small stable of not very good leftish academics who oppose it. (Some writers are now passing themselves off as economists.)

The truth is that most economists know more about Canadian literature than our writers know about economics.

In recent exchanges between Richard Lipsey, the very distinguished Canadian economist, and some of the leftist opponents of free trade, the poverty of thought of the opponents is all too obvious.

If one poses the question: "What is your alternative to the free trade deal?" the answers are a combination of vagueness and emotion.

What would the opponents put in place of the dispute settlement mechanism that has been worked out? Well, nothing, actually.

They would rest on the status quo, forgetting it is precisely the likelihood of widespread Congressional attacks on individual industries that present such a threat to Canada. There is no status quo to go back to.

Instead of a broad-based deal, the opponents would revert to the ideal of sectoral agreements. Which sectors? Why, like the Auto Pact!

Those same people forget that they opposed the Auto Pact in the first place, and that the free trade deal has preserved the benefits of the Auto Pact to Canada. And without the free trade deal, the Auto Pact might not survive.

The opponents of the deal would prefer to rely on the General Agreement on Tariffs and Trade (GATT).

This preference is based on the quite ludicrous assumption that it would be easier to negotiate with the European Community and the Japanese than with the Americans. The treatment of Canadian agriculture by the EC shows where we stand on that score.

In their determination to be unrealistic and impractical, the opponents of the deal have overlooked the fact that the GATT has brought two rulings (on wine and West Coast fish processing), the first being more severe than would have been the case under the free trade deal and the second being part of the deal with the U.S. Why do they think that the GATT will be more flexible than the Americans?

The opponents say they would either tear up the deal or write it a different way. A different government might appoint different negotiators and set different objectives, though it is hard to see what.

Perhaps the opponents might also tell us how they would persuade the Americans to set a different American agenda, and appoint a more amicable set of American negotiators. Does anyone suppose that presenting the Americans with a more nationalistic and intransigent negotiating position would soften the American approach or change American objectives?

In the past 50 years, we have moved from being a somewhat colonial dominion (the word is now dead), to being a reasonably autonomous democracy. Our trade with the U.S. has increased both absolutely and relatively, and it has also become free of tariff and non-tariff barriers.

The argument that there is a high correlation between economic interdependence and loss of cultural identity is simply inconsistent with the facts.

It seems to me that the Canadian public is beginning to see through the fog of emotion and bias that is being pumped out by the communications and cultural left.

It makes one wonder what our other economic policies would be if there were a more balanced presentation in the media.

Chapter twenty-four:
a beaver fights back
in a kangaroo court

Nicholas J. Patterson

Mr. Patterson is executive director of the Canadian Development Institute. From a presentation to the Ontario cabinet sub-committee on free trade, Ottawa, October 27, 1987.

If there was ever a time we needed some statesmanship in Ontario instead of low-brow political pandering to small, loud-mouth pressure groups, this is it.

We have a major economic crisis on our hands, with collapsing securities markets, a risk of depression, and worst of all, staring us straight in the eye, a disastrous round of U.S. protectionism, the very thing which, historians agree, was the most important factor in the last, worst depression in history, the dirty thirties, which scarred so many lives. And you people are against free trade with the U.S.! It's hard to believe, in these circumstances. But Peterson [Ontario Premier David Peterson] ran on this ticket and, worse still, shows no sign of coming to his senses, despite recent developments.

The Peterson government better wise up, and fast. And you people had better learn some economics. And you had better learn some history, too.

Why? Because you are playing politics with the future livelihood of Ontario.

You don't understand that we are facing a crisis of unprecedented proportions in this country. Your questions clearly show you don't understand a thing. I've never in my life heard so much nonsense coming from Ontario cabinet ministers, who should know better.

You guys are bleating about the bogeyman of foreign ownership, when in fact foreign ownership has been declining for 20 years, starting eight years before the Foreign Investment Review Agency was even thought of.

Talking about the fact that the free trade agreement isn't perfect — of course it's not perfect. But it is better than what we have now, with the Americans lowering the boom, every whipstich, on Canada, from lumber to steel, you name it. And you guys are talking about how some small sectors will be hurt, despite the substantial transition arrangements, and the fact that the vast majority of the economy will benefit with more jobs, a fact agreed by all objective experts.

This is all baloney in the context of the larger crisis we are facing — a catastrophic risk of depression, made worse by the prospect of losing access to the U.S. market.

And I'm very concerned about the integrity of these proceedings. For starters, your government put in a Deputy Minister of Industry, a guy named Pat Lavelle, in 1985. He's dead against free trade. But remember, he was dead against the Auto Pact, too. I spoke to him in 1981 about the Auto Pact, and he couldn't wait to catch his breath, about what a raw deal it was. Please, Pat Lavelle, give me a break!

Of course, everyone who knows anything realizes how good it was. Even the NDP, which opposed it for 20 years, now finally admits it was a good deal after all. It was a free-trade bonanza for Canada. We outperformed the Americans, and autos are now our largest single export, by a huge margin.

This committee itself, too, is just a one-sided, put-up job, a bunch of Liberal partisans against free trade, without an opportunity for a free trade point of view in your own councils. The reason is that if you had a free trade supporter in there, he would make a monkey out of your committee with his minority report. That is because the merits of free trade are clear as a bell, unanimously agreed to by the top economists in the land. A vast majority of businessmen, too, who know their own situations, have concluded that this deal means more business and more jobs.

The proceedings of this committee are a classic case of political hackmanship at its worst, particularly considering that your record as politicians is so lousy on economic matters. For example, you politicians ignored the landlords and their warnings about the effects of rent controls on the social fabric of our shelter economy. But you guys said, what do **they** know about their own business? You people knew it all!

And now you have made a massive screw up in the housing economy unprecedented in the history of Ontario. Mr. Sobara, you told me earlier today that Ontario has the best-housed people in the world. You are dead wrong! I suggest you read a book we published on this subject. We used to be the best housed, but you political hacks took that away from us with rent controls. One of the basics about a good housing economy, Mr. Sobara, is being able to find a place to live. And Ontario is the worst place in the industrial world today to find a place to rent. Dilapidation is now well entrenched in Toronto, with rent controls the leading cause, according to municipal officials. So please, Mr. Sobara, get your facts straight and cut the bull. And get your facts on free trade, too. You people have made the Davis Government look like pikers when it comes to screwing up our rental economy. And now you are going to do it on a wholesale basis by screwing up this free trade deal.

I say to you and to David Peterson: Wake up! Listen! And pay attention to people who know more.

You guys should listen to some experts, instead of just mainly the loud-mouth minority pressure groups which have, for some reason, been so prominent before your committee, along with a remarkable number of Liberal Party hacks. I don't want to suggest that you have manipulated the appearances before your phoney free trade committee. I'll leave that to NDPer Mike Cassidy, who said it very well. He said on TV that your committee sneaks into town in the dead of night, and sneaks out the following day.

Whatever the merits of that, I'd suggest you might want to seek some advice from people who know, such as experts at the Economic Council of Canada. I know for a fact they don't want to come before your committee, because they think it's a put up job and a waste of time. That is what one of their top people told me. Personally, I think that is a great mistake by them. In any event, let me suggest to you that you invite them specifically to attend, perhaps even subpoena them to attend. Why? Because they are experts. And because it is run by Judy Maxwell, who is one of the top economists in the country — and she has integrity, too!

But the Peterson government isn't interested in the facts, as put out by honest, professional experts with integrity. Why, the very first thing the Peterson government did, when you guys took office in 1985, was to disband the Economic Council of Ontario. Then you turned the matter of free trade over to a biased committee of partisan politicos, such as yourselves, supported by a bunch of phoney research reports. And the poor, benighted citizens of Ontario will pay the price of your political hacksmanship — not likely you people — rather the poor and unemployed.

David Peterson, even as a political cynic, has been duped. Why? Because he has succumbed to the left-wing, anti-American bandwagon, without realizing it is manipulated by a minority, mainly the NDP, along with that comic book of a newspaper, the **Toronto Star**, and a few fat-cat union bosses who don't even represent their members, for goodness sake. The latest poll, by Environics, shows that union members who support free trade far exceed those who don't. But union boss Bob White, with his anti-American NDP agenda, is busy criss-crossing the country anyway, spending their money — involuntarily forced union dues — whether they like it or not. That is a disgrace, too; one that will soon be unlawful, thank goodness. The irony, of course, is that his own salary is paid from the fruits of free trade, gained in the Auto Pact. He is your classic dog in the manger: "We've got it — but you can't have it." And it is a good fat salary, too, for a guy who never worked a day in his life in an auto plant.

And then you have the phoney research studies against free trade coming out of the Peterson government these days, at a great rate. The last one, heavily touted by Premier Dave in the media, was a real gut-buster — a classic in the "pass the nuts" department. He actually said, with a straight face, that free trade was a major women's issue!

> **The beaver is "noted for its habit, as a fighter, of biting off its testicals and offering them to its pursuer." Thank you, Margaret Atwood, for that artistic insight into the complexities of free trade.**

Why? Because, according to him, over 100,000 women are going to lose their jobs in our clothing and textile industry, from free trade. This figure itself, of course, is baloney, because this loss — if there is one — will be made up many times over by new jobs created elsewhere for these workers by free trade.

But worse is that Peterson, as a political hustler, failed to point out the flip side of the so-called women's issue of clothing and textiles. This is the fact that all Canadian women and their families are major beneficiaries of free trade, because they are finally going to get an honest break on clothing prices, for the first time in decades. This is after a generation of scandalous, artificially high prices, as a result of protecting a few fat-cat corporations.

These fat cats and their over-paid, hell-raising unionized employees have been ripping off Canadian consumers for decades with over-priced clothing, behind a protective wall of high tariffs and import quotas, and — worst of all — hundreds of millions of dollars of government grants, year after year for decades. These leeches continue to claim they need just a few more years of protection and just a few more millions in grants, before they can finally make their plants competitive. But it is always next year. Their appetite for feeding at the public teat has proven insatiable. Enough! Thank goodness this is going to stop and the women of Canada are finally going to get an honest break, particularly the poor, who suffer most from artificially high clothing prices.

But David Peterson, he doesn't want that. No, no, he would rather continue the textile-clothing protection racket, that costs the poor the most. He tries to pretend he is a socialist, bringing the Liberal Party of Ontario to the left — but it is ringing pretty hollow from a guy who is against cheaper clothing for the poor!

The other irony of all this is that freer trade with the United States requires no "leap of faith" at all. I believe that Donald Macdonald, who used this phrase, was taken out of context. The simple, bald fact is that all the leading economists in the world, virtually without exception, know that freer trade is always beneficial to any national economy fortunate enough to have it. History shows this, and economic theory shows it, too.

In any event, the well respected Economic Council of Canada has clearly established that the vast majority, 29 out of 32, of major industries in Canada would benefit from freer trade — the vast majority of the economy, and employment too. And the Council has shown that the net new job creation would be in excess of 300,000 jobs. These people know what they are talking about because they are the top people in their field. Judy Maxwell is no hack. She wouldn't say it just because David Peterson told her to, or because Brian Mulroney told her to, either. Her study confirms, beyond a doubt, that freer trade means a great many new jobs and greater prosperity for all Canadians.

But that doesn't cut any ice with you people, because I asked a couple of you earlier, and all I got was a bunch of lame duck nit-pics about report. Baloney!

So I don't expect you will pay any attention to all the other experts, either, namely the vast majority of patriotic Canadian businessmen, who know for sure their own industries will benefit — and gain many more jobs, too. Why? Because they know their business, damn it! And the vast majority of them are 100 percent behind free trade.

But you people would rather go with the loud-mouth minority groups and subsidized culture vultures. Novelist Margaret Atwood told the Commons committee on free trade the other day that the beaver was "noted for its habit, as a fighter, of biting off its testicles and offering them to its pursuer" — obviously an important artistic insight into this complex issue. Thank you, Margaret Atwood!

You people should, of course, listen to such trade experts as Margaret Atwood — but don't ignore the economists and the business community — because they know more than you guys do. And for heavens sake, stop playing low-brow politics with the future livelihood of Ontario in these perilous times. And you should be careful, too, because otherwise you might suffer the revenge of the beaver — the one that free trade expert Margaret Atwood described so graphically.

Thank you for pretending to listen to one who would still be proud to be described as an energetic and even, perhaps, an angry Canadian beaver, especially when provoked by your phoney free trade debate committee.

PART SIX:
THE INTERESTS
OF WOMEN

Chapter twenty-five:
an opportunity to
adjust things better

Katie MacMillan

Ms. MacMillan is a consulting economist who has worked for the C.D. Howe Institute, the Economic Council of Canada, and the Canada West Foundation. From a submission to the House of Commons Standing Committee on External Affairs and International Trade, Ottawa, November 19, 1987.

By way of introduction, I was responsible for one of three papers that was commissioned by the Canadian Advisory Council on the Status of Women on this particular issue. I am an economist, and I have worked with the Economic Council of Canada and the Canada West Foundation. I am currently working on a part-time basis with the C.D. Howe Institute. I would like to state quite clearly, however, that I am not here as a representative of any of these organizations; I am speaking only as an author of the advisory council paper.

Canadian women have a particular stake in free trade, and it goes beyond the genuine interest we have in the direction of our economic future. Because women tend to feel disadvantaged in our labor market, we are concerned with the possible adjustments arising from free trade and whether they would work to our benefit or to our detriment. The Ontario government, through its women's directorate and other anti-free trade lobbyists, has been very effective in creating the impression that Canadian women have a great deal to fear from free trade.

I have two objections to this point of view. First, I strongly believe that the evidence leads to quite the opposite conclusion. Secondly, I note that they do not provide any constructive alternatives that would improve the situation of women workers in Canada.

Canadian women currently earn on average two-thirds the wages of men. We are also very poorly represented in those occupations offering the best incomes and the most promising career opportunities. Those opposed to free trade are simply offering us the status quo in dealing with the realities that we face in the workplace.

The time available to me is very short, and because the Ontario government and others have had the benefit of a great deal of attention in the media on this issue, I feel my time would be most constructively used to address seven of their basic assertions.

First, they assert that most jobs held by women would be in jeopardy under free trade. The truth is that most women workers would be completely unaffected. Four-fifths of Canadian women in the labor force work in the service sector, and the majority of those are in industries referred to as non-trade services. They include things like education, health care, public administration, and personal services. The jobs of those workers and those employed in the primary sector of our economy would not be eliminated by free trade with the U.S.

Various studies have predicted that substantial employment gains would arise from free trade. Women in the service sector in particular would see their employment prospects vastly improved as a result of greater consumer spending and investment accompanying free trade. Less than 12 percent of the Canadian female labor force is employed in manufacturing, and this is where the bulk of the trade adjustment would occur. The Ontario government, for one, is of the belief that tens of thousands of women manufacturing workers are threatened by free trade. This is based on the observation that female manufacturing employment is more concentrated in those industries considered to be most sensitive to import pressure.

It is important to point out, however, that male jobs in those so-called trade sensitive industries outnumber female jobs by almost two to one. Insofar as adjustment is required in those industries, the number would suggest that twice as many men would be affected. As I will argue later, saying that an industry is import-competing is a far cry from saying that it would lose all its jobs as a result of free trade with the United States.

Secondly, we have the assertion that a number of our manufacturing industries simply would not survive free trade with the U.S. There are various reasons for believing this is not the case. Analysis of trading arrangements such as the European free trade area have shown that specialization and rationalization mainly occur within industries and not between industries. This was certainly Canada's experience with the two major rounds of tariff reductions under the GATT, the Kennedy round and the Tokyo round.

Examination of that experience found that virtually every Canadian industry increased both exports and imports relative to domestic production during the period of trade liberalization. This occurred because Canadian industries specialized in particular niches which caused trading volumes to rise in both directions. Removing the final 10 percent tariffs existing between our two countries will not wipe out entire industries in Canada.

The Economic Council of Canada's analysis even found that the industry considered the most sensitive to bilateral free trade, the footwear industry, would have its employment levels only 6.2 percent lower by 1995 than those expected to exist without free trade. We will survive by specializing in the production of what we do best. Examples from the clothing industry would include things like high-fashion clothing and winter outer-wear.

Another example we can look to is the Canadian textile industry, which has gone on record in support of free trade. That industry has demonstrated its confidence and its ability to compete by undertaking capital investments of $1.4 billion over the past four years. This year the industry will invest $400 million, more than it has ever invested before.

Let us also remember that U.S. tariffs that are high in these same industries would be also removed under a free trade deal and the phase-in period would be as much as 10 years for heavily protected industries.

Thirdly, we hear the suggestion that free trade with the U.S. poses the only threat to jobs in the so-called trade sensitive manufacturing industries. Free trade opponents are frequently guilty of confusing general import sensitivity with sensitivity to free trade with the United States. The same industries identified as being at a competitive disadvantage in the North American market are being subjected to even greater competitive pressures from the newly industrialized countries. When we try to compete with low-wage countries, we impose a burden on taxpayers and consumers, who must pay for the protection these industries require, and on workers in those industries, many of whom are women.

Fourthly, the assumption is made that Canadian women are quite satisfied working in jobs most men would find unacceptable. It is often said that women would face big adjustments under a free trade arrangement. While this might be the case, I would like to point out that women have borne the costs of many years of decisions not to adjust our industries in the face of pressures to do so.

Many women in manufacturing are dependent on jobs that are least attractive in terms of wages, working conditions, skill levels and possibilities for advancement. If offered an alternative, I do not believe many Canadian women would choose to stay in these occupations, nor would they recommend them to their daughters. Our efforts would be much better devoted to easing the adjustment of women out of some of these areas. Perhaps the most significant accomplishments of free trade would be to provide Canadian women with an opportunity to move to better jobs in more promising sectors of our economy.

Fifthly, we have the claim that women do not adjust well to changes in employment. Perhaps it is worthwhile to put the issue of adjustment in some context. Approximately one million Canadians lost full-time jobs and were not recalled between 1981 and 1984. In the three years between September 1984 and August 1987, 900,000 new jobs, jobs which did not exist before, were created in our economy. The issue is not whether job loss and job creation is a good or bad thing, because clearly it goes on all the time. The question for Canadian women is firstly, the difficulties posed by labor adjustment, and secondly whether job adjustment can work to our advantage.

New evidence exists, based on labor force surveys conducted by Statistics Canada, that challenges traditional views on women and labor force adjustment. The survey findings suggest that on average displaced women workers are unemployed for shorter periods of time than men and in contrast to men they experience an increase in earnings when they move to a new job. Of course we all know this is largely because women have nowhere to go but up. I suppose this, in a nutshell, is part of the message I am trying to convey.

The issue of adjustment is key to the question of women and free trade. I am not going to deny that job losses will occur initially and they will particularly affect those women the least advantaged in our labor market. I for one would like to see a comprehensive adjustment package containing programs especially geared to the unique requirements of women workers. Although research has shown that women are more resilient in job displacement than many would lead us to believe, and that we could actually improve our economic circumstances as a result of it, we desperately need measures to help women leave poor jobs in declining areas and move to growing sectors of our economy.

Finally, I would like to talk about the assertion that women as consumers would not benefit from free trade with the U.S. I am aware this very point has been argued before your committee. This assertion flies in the face of economic reality. It also displays an inconsistency inherent in the arguments against free trade, that industries will lay off workers because of increased competition but they somehow will be able to maintain or even increase selling prices in spite of that competition. If they are telling us prices will be the same, then they are also telling us we will not face any of the job adjustments I spoke of earlier. It is obviously not possible to have it both ways.

Women have a particular interest in the consumer savings arising from free trade. This is all women we are talking about, including those unable to work outside the home or those who choose not to work outside the home. High tariff and non-tariff barriers especially hurt women since a greater share of our income tends to go towards the purchase of basic necessities, such as clothing or food, which are more expensive as a result.

In conclusion, free trade offers Canadian women the chance to improve our economic circumstances both as workers and as consumers. Women have not been served well by our existing industrial structure, since we incur the greatest cost of protecting jobs in industries that compete with low-wage countries. Virtually every analysis on this subject has concluded that free trade would expand Canadian incomes and create employment opportunities. This would allow women to leave jobs with no future for jobs with a future. I believe programs should exist to assist women in this transition and to help us realize our true potential.

Who can you read in Canadian Speeches?

The Governor General, the Prime Minister, bank chairmen, university presidents, labor leaders, Nobel prize winners, premiers, cabinet minister, authors, educators, lawyers, doctors. These are among the people whose speeches are published in **Canadian Speeches.** People like David Suzuki, David Peterson, Judith Maxwell, John Sewell. Alphabetically, the list reads from the Aga Kahn to Roger Young of the North-South Institute. On the political spectrum, the names of those whose speeches we have published range from Shirley Carr on the left to Barbara Amiel on the right.

Ten issues per year, with the texts of 10 to 13 speeches in each issue. No advertising. The most informed thought on the most important issues.

We're looking for informed and well-articulated speeches that present diverse and decisive views on current topics of national interest. Every text submitted will be carefully considered for publication (we reserve the right to edit).

Available by subscription, $65 per year, with a discount of $20 available to high schools, colleges, universities and public libraries.

For a free sample copy, write to **Canadian Speeches,** PO box 250, Woodville, Ontario, K0M 2T0.